BULLETIN OF MILWAUKEE PUBLIC MUSEUM

Volume 2, Number 4, March 1933

MIWOK MATERIAL CULTURE

By

S. A. Barrett and E. W. Gifford

INDIAN LIFE
of the Yosemite Region

Published by the Yosemite Association

Yosemite National Park, California

ISBN 0-939666-12-X

MIWOK MATERIAL CULTURE

CONTENTS

ILLUSTRATIONS

Plates[1]

[1]In the "Explanation of Plate" accompanying each individual plate, the N. C, and S after specimen numbers indicate respectively Northern, Central and Southern Miwok. Except as otherwise stated, specimen numbers refer to specimens in the University of California Museum of Anthropology.

Text Figures

Maps

INTRODUCTION

The Miwok proper who occupied a considerable section of the Sierra Nevada range of mountains, together with their western foothills and a relatively small portion of the adjacent Sacramento-San Joaquin Valley in California,[1a] came into contact at a relatively early time with the whites. Both in the "Mission period" and during the gold rush of "49" their numbers were heavily depleted and their culture suffered greatly. Hence it was with difficulty that information was obtained concerning some features of the Miwok culture. The data on which this paper is based were obtained from Miwok informants during field trips in behalf of the University of California in and after 1906.

In addition to the collections of the University of California Museum of Anthropology from which most of our detailed studies of Miwok specimens were made, there was also made available to the authors the Miwok material in the Field Museum of Natural History and the Peabody Museum of American Archaeology and Ethnology at Harvard University. Our appreciation of these courtesies is here acknowledged. All specimens numbers preceded by 1- indicate that the objects are in the University of California Museum.

The orthography employed is that set forth in a previous paper on this same group.[1b]

Thanks are especially due to Professors W. A. Setchell, N. L. Gardner, and H. M. Hall, and to Miss Alice Eastwood for the identification of plants.

[1a]See Maps 2 and 3.
[1b]S. A. Barrett, 1908, 359-361. For full citations see bibliography.

ENVIRONMENT

The Miwok, one of the five Penutian stocks of California, are divided into six dialectic groups. Two of these groups are not considered in this paper, namely, the Coast Miwok of Marin county and the Lake Miwok of Lake county. The four groups discussed comprise the Plains Miwok of the Sacramento-San Joaquin delta region, and the Northern, Central, and Southern Miwok of the foothills and mountains of the Sierra Nevada, between El Dorado county in the north and Madera county in the south. These latter three are collectively designated as Sierra Miwok in this paper. What little is known of Coast and Lake Miwok cultures indicates that they resembled Pomo culture rather than the culture of the Plains and Sierra Miwok.

With the establishment of the Spanish missions in the latter part of the eighteenth century, and especially with the settlement of southern and central California shortly thereafter, the Miwok were brought more or less into contact with the whites. This contact was not so serious as the more intimate one to which the coast tribes were subjected. However, owing to the peonage system more or less in vogue among the settlers, the Miwok, like other groups even in northern California, were frequently disturbed by raids.

In June, 1848, six months before the great gold rush to California began, the penetration of the Sierra Nevada Miwok territory began. A man named Woods discovered gold in Woods' creek near Jamestown, Tuolumne county, in the territory of the Central Miwok. From the gold rush, during 1849 and the following years, the Miwok were perhaps the greatest sufferers, because the principal gold-bearing regions lay in their territory. The native culture was thus disrupted relatively early, so that many customs and utensils have become matters of memory among even the older people.

The territory occupied by the Plains and Sierra Miwok may be divided into three regions: the delta and plains of the Great valley proper, the foothills, and the mountains. The only Miwok in the valley were those in the plains and delta between Sacramento and Stockton.[2] This group spoke the Plains dialect. Here were rush bordered sloughs and lagoons, thickly populated with waterfowl and deep water fishes,

---

[2]For discussion of distribution see Merriam, 1907; Kroeber, 1908.

such as sturgeon. Certain peculiar cultural features existed here: the tule-thatched house, tule balsa, and special fishing appliances. This highly desirable agricultural region earliest felt the full impact of Caucasian culture, so that the native culture vanished before that in the hills and mountains.

The three remaining dialects, Northern, Central, and Southern, were confined to the grassy or bushy, but comparatively open, foothills, and to the wooded mountains of the Sierra Nevada. Both these environments also developed appropriate cultural features, such as the grass thatched and the bark-slab house, respectively. These differentiations occurred from west to east and were therefore largely correlated with altitude and life zone. Within any given range of altitude, or floral belt, little cultural difference was to be found from north to south through the whole Miwok region. Minor peculiarities among the Northern and Southern Miwok seem explainable as due to Maidu and Yokuts influences. The western frontier of Central and Southern Miwok territory seems to have been the junction of the lower foothills with the valley. Linguistic and topographic boundaries thus corresponded.

Above 4000 feet the Sierra winter is so snowy that the Miwok seasonally moved to lower altitudes. Included in the higher Miwok territory was Yosemite valley. It was the resort, in summer, of the adjacent Miwok, and of parties of Washo and Mono who came from the east to trade. A few Miwok seem to have resided there the year round.

Of greater importance culturally than the dialectic differences among the Miwok are the life zones of the Miwok habitat. These run north and south and cut across the dialectic boundaries, as do also the climatic boundaries. See maps 2 and 3.[3] The easterly Plains Miwok lived along the rivers in the Lower Sonoran zone, the westerly in the Upper Sonoran of the Delta, chiefly regions of hot summer Mediterranean climate. The three Sierra divisions occupied the Lower Sonoran, Upper Sonoran, and Transition zones, regions respectively of hot steppe, hot summer Mediterranean, and intermediate Mediterranean climates. The first zone embraces the Sierra Nevada foothills up to about 1000 feet elevation. The second zone embraces the mountains from about 1000 to 3000 feet elevation, and 4000 feet on south-facing slopes. Residence sites within the Transition zone were probably not numerous.

---

[3]Cf. Merriam, 1914.

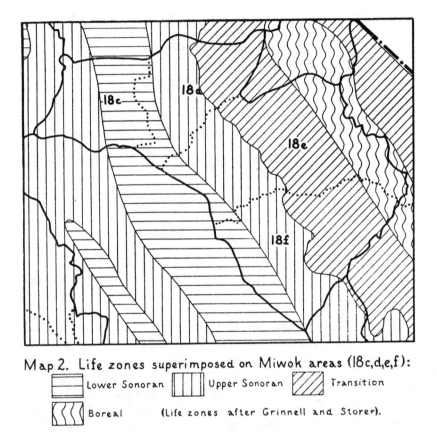

Map 2. Life zones superimposed on Miwok areas (18c,d,e,f):

| Lower Sonoran | Upper Sonoran | Transition |
| Boreal | (Life zones after Grinnell and Storer). |

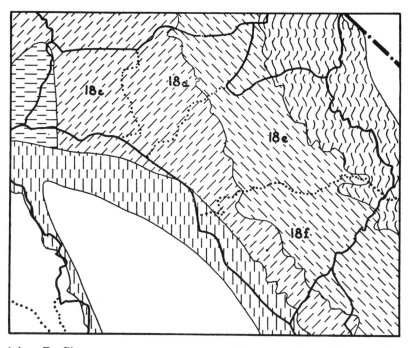

Map 3. Climates superimposed on Miwok areas (18 c,d,e,f):

 Cool Summer Mediterranean

Hot Steppe

Hot Summer Mediterranean

Microthermal

Intermediate between Cool and Hot Summer Mediterranean

(Climates after Russell)

Peculiar plants of the river bottoms in the Lower Sonoran of the east side of the San Joaquin valley are Fremont cottonwoods and valley oaks. At a representative point, such as Snelling (elevation 250 feet), in Southern Miwok territory, the following animals are peculiar to this zone in the breeding season: Mockingbird, Texas Nighthawk, Blue Grosbeak, Dwarf Cowbird, Fresno Pocket Gopher, Merced Kangaroo Rat, Golden Beaver, and other exclusively warm-belt types of animals.[4]

The Upper Sonoran may be recognized by the presence of digger pines, buckeyes, blue oaks, interior live oaks, and by a host of bushy plants which constitute the "California chaparral." Along the Merced river in Southern Miwok territory this zone extends from Merced Falls (elevation *ca.* 500 feet), some fifty miles up the river to El Portal (elevation 2000 feet). Some of its distinctive species of animals are California Jay, Northern Brown Towhee, Pallid Wren-tit, Plain Titmouse, California Thrasher, California Bush-tit, San Joaquin Wren, Hutton Vireo, Anna Hummingbird, Western Gnat-catcher, Bell Sparrow, Rufous-crowned Sparrow, Dusky Poor-will, Nuttall Woodpecker, Mariposa Brush Rabbit, Gilbert White-footed Mouse, Parasitic White-footed Mouse, Mariposa Meadow Mouse, Digger Pine Pocket Gopher, Heermann Kangaroo Rat, San Diego Alligator Lizard, and California Striped Racer.

In the Transition zone the blue-green of the digger pine yields to the deeper green of the western yellow pine. The change from one tree to the other is a marked one, apparent to the most casual observer. Other characteristic Transition zone trees are the Douglas spruce, golden oak, black oak, and incense cedar. On the walls of Yosemite valley this zone rises to about the 6000-foot level. A few upper Sonoran birds and mammals reach up into the Transition, but for the most part an entirely new set predominates. But few of these are absolutely restricted to this zone; the greater number range farther upward. The more distinctively Transition vertebrates are: Band-tailed Pigeon, California Purple Finch, Black-throated Gray Warbler, Calaveras Warbler, Western Flycatcher, Black Swift, Pigmy Owl, Northern Spotted Owl, Northwestern Long-legged Bat, Boyle White-footed Mouse, Yosemite Pocket Gopher, and Coral King Snake. Some well-known species which range down into the Transition from zones above are: Blue-fronted Jay, Western Robin, Sierra Junco, Sierra Creeper, Short-tailed

[4]Lists of species are derived from Grinnell and Storer, 1921, 125-131, and 1924, 11, 12.

Mountain Chicadee, American Dipper, Sierra Hermit Thrush, Mountain Weasel, Yosemite Meadow Mouse, and Sierra Nevada Flying Squirrel.

At about the 6000-foot contour a rather impressive change is again to be noted; the golden oak is replaced by the dwarf huckleberry oak, the California laurel and maple and black oak disappear, the Jeffrey pine replaces the yellow pine, and red firs and aspens appear. These mark the Canadian Zone, the lowest of the three zones constituting the Boreal of our map 2. Birds encountered here are: Yosemite Fox Sparrow, Williamson Sapsucker, Sierra Grouse, Townsend Solitaire, Western Ruby-crowned Kinglet, Red-breasted Nuthatch, Cassin Purple Finch, California Evening Grosbeak, Lincoln Sparrow, Hammond Flycatcher, and Western Goshawk. Among the mammals are: Navigator Shrew, Pacific Fisher, Allen Jumping Mouse, Yellow-haired Porcupine, Sierra Mountain Beaver, Sierra Golden-mantled Ground Squirrel, Tahoe Chipmunk, Allen Chipmunk, and Sierra Chickaree. Here also are the Tenaya Blue-bellied Lizard, Mountain Lizard, and Sierra Alligator Lizard.

The Hudsonian Zone is the belt of forest just below timberline. It contains the lodgepole pine, which occurs commonly in the Canadian Zone, and has also trees of its own, namely alpine hemlock, silver pine, and white-bark pine. Birds become scarcer in this zone, though mammals remain plentiful; some of the species extend up from the zone below. The California Pine Grosbeak, Mountain Bluebird, White-crowned Sparrow, Alpine Chipmunk, Belding Ground Squirrel, Sierra Marmot, Mountain Lemming Mouse, Gray Bushy-tailed Wood Rat, Yosemite Cony, Sierra White-tailed Jack-rabbit, Pine Marten, Wolverine, and Sierra Least Weasel are rather closely restricted to it.

The Arctic-Alpine is the highest of all the zones and covers the treeless area from about the 10,500-foot contour to the summits of the loftiest peaks. Only one species of bird is confined to it, the Sierra Nevada Rosy Finch. Some of the Hudsonian mammals enter it locally; for example, Gray Bushy-tailed Wood Rat, Yosemite Cony, and Alpine Chipmunk.

It must be kept in mind that many of the vertebrate animals are not so closely restricted as the ones named in the preceding paragraphs. Certain species range regularly through two zones, for example, the Blue-fronted Jay; a few through three zones, as with the Sierra Junco. In exceptional cases as many as five out of the six zones named are covered, as is done by the Red-shafted Flicker, Sparrow Hawk, and Western Chipping Sparrow.

The restriction of animals by "zones" applies particularly to the breeding season. Migratory species of both birds and mammals range more or less widely at other times of the year according to food requirements. Close adaptation of a species to a kind of food supply which disappears at the close of the summer season makes necessary search elsewhere for it in the winter.

Inasmuch as the material culture is dependent upon the raw materials which nature offers, it follows that the most striking cultural differences are correlated with the life and climatic zones. Thus the material culture areas of the Sierra Miwok groups may be thought of as comprising three long parallel bands, stretching from north to south right across the three dialectic areas.

The Plains Miwok of the Upper and Lower Sonoran zones constitute a fourth culture division, that of the Delta and Plains of the Lower Sacramento and San Joaquin rivers. The plains lie to the eastward of the swampy delta. The plains lie in the lower Sonoran, the swamps in the upper Sonoran.

Our picture of the material culture of the Plains Miwok is the least complete, because of the early replacement of the Indian population by the Caucasians. However, the fragmentary nature of our ethnological data is offset in considerable measure by the excellent account of the archaeology of the region by Schenck and Dawson.[5] They describe the ancient culture of the Plains Miwok and northernmost Yokuts areas.

Although residence in this or that life zone largely colored the material culture of the Miwok of a given elevation, whether they were Northern, Central, or Southern in dialect, it did not prevent them from availing themselves to some extent of the products of the adjacent life zones above and below them. Thus the Upper Sonoran zone people obtained Lower Sonoran valley products by trade or by making excursions into the valley to hunt antelope and other characteristic valley animals. Similarly, the Transition zone mountain people might visit in summer the Canadian zone for sugar pine nuts and other characteristic products. They now and then penetrated the Hudsonian zone, but presumably never the Arctic-Alpine.

---

[5]Schenck and Dawson, 1929.

Permanent residence did not extend above the Transition zone.   In the Canadian and Hudsonian zones only summer camps were made.

In the steep, deep canyons, such as those of the Tuolumne and Stanislaus rivers, it was possible for Miwok with permanent villages at the edge of the Transition zone, as at Tuolumne, to climb down the canyon walls and reach the Upper Sonoran fauna and flora at the canyon bottom in an hour.   The villages in the mountains were habitually on the ridges, not in the canyons.   A spring or small stream, and not the river, was the source of water supply for such a village.

In the Lower Sonoran foothill country, villages were often near the river, as the canyons of the great rivers were there much shallower.

Map 3 shows the climates of the Miwok habitat.   The climatic areas coincide rather closely with the life zones, as might be expected.

Associations of topographic and botanic features in the several zones are as follows:

ASSOCIATIONS WITHIN THE LOWER SONORAN ZONE[6]

Open-water (two types, River and Slough)	Rose-thicket
Riparian (Willow-cottonwood)	Valley-oak
Marsh	Hog-wallow prairie
Meadow	Rock outcrop

ASSOCIATIONS WITHIN THE UPPER SONORAN ZONE

Stream	Digger-pine
Riparian (Willow)	Blue-oak
Meadow	Dry grassland
Live-oak	Rocky-slope
Chaparral (two types, *Adenostoma* and *Ceanothus cuneatus*)	

ASSOCIATIONS WITHIN THE TRANSITION ZONE

Swift-stream	Black-oak
Riparian (two types, Willow-cottonwood and Alder)	Golden-oak
Meadow	Yellow-pine
Dry Grassland	Silver-fir
Chaparral (two types, Sticky-manzanita and Buckthorn)	Boulder-talus
	Cliff

ASSOCIATIONS WITHIN THE CANADIAN ZONE

Swift-stream	Red-fir
Riparian (two types, Willow and *Cornus pubescens*)	Lodgepole-pine
Aspen	Jeffrey-pine
Meadow	Granite outcrop
Chaparral (three types, Red-cherry, *Arctostaphylos patula*, and Huckleberry-oak)	Cliff

ASSOCIATIONS WITHIN THE HUDSONIAN ZONE

Lake	Lodgepole-pine
Shore	Hemlock
Swift-stream	Whitebark-pine
Riparian (Willow)	Talus (or Rock-slide)
Meadow	Cliff
Heather	

ASSOCIATIONS WITHIN THE ARCTIC-ALPINE ZONE

Swift-stream	Dry grassland
Willow-thicket	Talus (Rock-slide)
Meadow	Cliff

[6]Grinnell and Storer, 1924, 11.

Places within Miwok territory lie in the different life zones (L, Lower Sonoran; U, Upper Sonoran; T, Transition), as follows: Plains Miwok: Lodi (U), Lockford (L). Northern Miwok: Ione (L), Jackson (U), Campo Seco (U), Mokelumne Hill (T), West Point (T). Central Miwok: Knights Ferry (L), La Grange (L), Angels Camp (U), Jamestown (U), Sonora (U), Tuolumne (T), Murphys (T). Southern Miwok: Merced Falls (L), Coulterville (U), Baxter (U), Hornitos (U), Bear Valley (U), Hite Cove (U), El Portal (U), Yosemite (T), Mariposa (T), Oakhurst (T).

The following tabulation attempts to correlate in a general way the cultural features of the Northern, Central, and Southern Miwok with life zones in the Sierra Nevada region, listing the features predominating in each zone.

	LOWER SONORAN	UPPER SONORAN	TRANSITION
House covering	Tule	Digger pine bark	Yellow pine bark / Big-tree bark
Pine nuts		Digger pine	Sugar pine
Principal food mammals	Antelope	Deer	Deer
	Jack rabbit	Jack rabbit	Gray squirrel
Salt	From ponds	From springs	From Mono
Principal food birds	Ducks	Valley quail	Mountain quail
	Geese		Pigeons
Principal food fish	Salmon		Trout
Women's skirts	Tule	Grass	Grass
Insect foods	Grasshoppers		Chrysalids
Beverage		Manzanita cider	
Nets	Duck	Rabbit	
Fences		Deer	Quail
Harpoon	Present		Absent
Acorns	Valley oak	Blue oak	Black oak
		Interior live oak	
Other vegetable foods	Seeds predominate (?)	Buckeye	Bulbs predominate (?)
Fish net	Seine, casting	Set net	Dip net
Blanket	Feather, rabbitskin		Fur
Navigation	Balsa	Logs	

FOODS AND MEDICINES

The food quest tied the Miwok more closely to their environment than did any other phase of culture. They levied widely upon the plant and animal worlds for their sustenance, for they were neither agriculturists nor herdsmen. Tobacco was the only plant cultivated, the dog the only animal domesticated. The plants and animals enumerated as food and medicine in the following pages by no means exhaust the list of life forms used. Apparently almost everything edible in the vegetable world was eaten.   Moreover, seasonal movements to different altitudes considerably amplified the diet.

With the extensive utilization of wild plant foods and of those animals most easily caught went a lowly material culture, a combination which seems common the world over among the most primitive groups. Food specialization is usually coupled with general advance in culture, as well as specifically with cultivation of plants and domestication of animals.

Of vegetable foods manzanita berries were the "cheapest" and least desirable.   Bulbs, corms, and mushrooms were next highest in ascending order of esteem.   Certain seeds came next, but were considered luxuries.   Acorns were regarded as the finest vegetable food.   The person who had a sufficiency of both acorns and venison was considered well off.   Black oak acorns and *Godetia viminea* seeds were the two most prized vegetable foods.   Deer meat was the most highly regarded flesh, with the meat of the California Gray Squirrel (me'we, C)[7] a close second.   In the lower foothills salmon was the most prized fish, in the mountains trout.

The principal crops were as follows: mushrooms in winter, clover in spring, seeds in summer, acorns in fall.   Plums and cherries were gathered between the seed harvest and the acorn harvest.   Bulbs were gathered in the spring.   In winter the diet was more largely of meat than at any other time of the year.   The mammals, especially squirrels, were fat and nice to eat at that season.

Nearly all the mammals, birds, reptiles, and fishes, which could be caught, served as food, as did several kinds of insects.   The carrion-feeding turkey vulture was the only bird specifically designated as not edible.   Among at least some of the Central Miwok bears were not eaten, because the "bear's foot looks too human."   These same people, however, ate the mountain lion, wild cat, coyote, dog, and skunk.[8]   The Southern Miwok ate the bullsnake and the striped watersnake, but the flesh of the rattlesnake was used only as medicine.   Among the Central Miwok rattlesnakes, gopher snakes, frogs, and lizards were eaten by old people.

[7]P, N, C, and S, after native words, indicate the dialectic groups: Plains, Northern, Central, and Southern.
[8]In spite of what Powers says to the contrary. Powers, 351.

The feet of the Mud Hen (*Fulica americana*) were tapu as food. Birds' eggs were not ordinarily eaten, but occasionally duck or quail eggs were roasted in ashes.

COOKING

Except for breakfast, which was eaten at sunrise, meals were not eaten at regular times. People ate when they felt hungry. Visitors were fed immediately upon their arrival. The term for breakfast is walus (N). Waluma (N) means to get breakfast. Apparently, these terms are derived from the term walisu (N), meaning daylight. The term uwu'a (N) means to eat. No spoons, except occasionally of river mussel shell, or other implements appear to have been used to convey the food to the mouth.

Stone boiling in baskets, boiling in steatite vessels, baking or steaming in the earth oven, parching with hot coals in a basket, broiling over coals, and roasting in hot ashes and coals were the principal methods of cooking. The following terms apply to these processes:

tcusu (C), to boil with hot stones in a basket.

yatcu (N), yatce (C), to parch in a basket.

ulup (N), ulu (C), to cook with steam in the earth oven, without a fire built on top. Earth oven, kume (P, N), ulup (N), ulu (C).

hubuya (N), to cook in the earth oven with the aid of a fire built on top.

hupu (C), to cook in hot coals or ashes.

hina (C), to broil on hot coals, as a salmon.

The larger mammals were skinned and sliced with the obsidian knife, and broiled on the coals of the open fire,[9] though sometimes boiled. The smaller mammals were sometimes roasted directly on coals or in hot ashes, either whole or skinned and eviscerated. In the latter case coals were placed inside to make the cooking more rapid and even. The fresh skins of various mammals were singed, then cooked in hot coals, which caused them to pop open. Tidbits were then nibbled from the crackling.

Birds and fishes were usually roasted whole in the ashes, and picked or skinned after cooking. Sometimes they were opened first and live coals placed within to facilitate the cooking.

---

[9]Horse meat was cooked in this fashion, after the animal had been introduced by the whites.

One method of cooking dried fish was to smear them with acorn mush and broil them on sticks over a fire. Acorn "biscuits" were eaten with the broiled fish.

Turtles were killed with a stone, then roasted in ashes, when they split open. The intestines were removed after roasting. Lizards (cakkadi, C) were gutted and roasted in hot ashes.

River mussels were cooked by sticking the mollusks in sand so that they projected, covering them with grass and brush, and igniting the inflammable material.

Bulbs, greens, and grasshoppers, were cooked in the earth oven, which was a pit in the ground. This was thoroughly heated and lined with a layer of hot stones, over which was placed a layer of green leaves, preferably of *Wyethia helenioides* (notopayu, C), sometimes grape leaves, *Vitis californica* (mū'te, P; mü'te, N; tolmesu, C), or green tule. Upon these a thin layer of the food was spread. This was covered with more leaves and then a layer of hot stones, then more leaves, more food, more stones, and so on until the pit was filled. Finally a layer of earth was heaped over the pit and often a fire built on top of it. The baking proceeded throughout the night, or sometimes for twenty-four hours. This oven, with the heated stones interspersed so as to evenly distribute the heat, would remain at a reasonable temperature for many hours, and the food would be hot and delicious almost any time during the following day. Sometimes water was poured around the edges of the oven in order to steam the food. If several families cooked in one oven the lots of food were separated.

Hot stones for boiling or baking were handled with two wooden sticks, pointed at one end. The pointed ends were used to hold the stones. The pair in Plate XXXI, figs, 6 and 7 are about five feet long and an inch in diameter. A second pair (1-9917) in the University's collection are about two feet long.

For old people with few or bad teeth dried meat and fish were pulverized in a mortar.

STORAGE OF FOODS

The Miwok by no means lived from hand to mouth, but preserved and stored large quantities of food. Acorns and seeds were stored without special preparation. Greens and grasshoppers were steamed and dried before packing away. Meat and fish were dried and stored.

Large, flat-bottomed, twined baskets (hupulu, C) were the containers most frequently used for foods other than acorns.

The meat of the large mammals, especially deer, was dried in long, thin strips, by either hanging it on trees or bushes to expose to the air and sunlight, or by curing on a babracot about eighteen inches above a small fire. Care was taken to remove all fat, which was kept in a small hupulu basket and eaten raw. One Central Miwok informant mentioned the storage of deer meat in a cedar-bark-lined pit, where it was mixed with salt and would keep for two or three weeks. It seems doubtful if the use of salt as a preservative is aboriginal. For temporary preservation between meals, meat was sometimes covered with earth.

Both mountain quail and valley quail, snared in large numbers in the spring, were dried for later consumption. The feathers were removed, and the breasts cut open, because too thick to dry properly otherwise. A sufficient quantity might thus be preserved to supply a family all summer. Although mourning doves were abundant, they were not preserved.

Fish of various kinds, especially whitefish, trout, and salmon, were dried and stored in hupulu baskets. The fish were dried whole if small, or eviscerated first if large. They were spread on bushes for four or five days; or exposed on a babracot to the heat and smoke of a small fire. If there were salt to spare it might be sprinkled on the fish. Nothing was placed between the layers of fish. The mountain dwellers above the range of the salmon sometimes went downstream to catch salmon.

THE USE OF PLANTS

The Miwok were not agriculturists, except so far as they grew a little tobacco. The only other control of vegetation which they attempted was the burning off of dry grass about August. This was said to have been done to get a better growth the following year. Underbrush was less abundant anciently than now, so informants said, and perhaps due to this periodic burning. What means, if any, were taken to prevent the spread of fire to trees was not learned. Forest fires no doubt were of frequent occurrence. "The Sierran forest is typically a fire forest; that is to say, all the tree species have shown reaction in structure or life history to long continued fires which have undoubtedly run over California woodlands for many thousands of years and perhaps for a longer period."[10]

Flowers in general are called loyema (C) ; bulbs and corms, olutcu (C) ; seeds, tū'yū (C, S) ; gum, takuta (C). Kelse (C) denotes certain bulbs or corms, with edible but insignificant roots, whose stems only are eaten. Three were mentioned (popkine, C; solasi, C; lippasi, C), but not identified.

Meals made from seeds are also called tū'yū (C, S). Some were eaten as dry meal, others in cake form, and still others were cooked as mush. The seeds were from grasses, other small plants, and shrubs. The conical burden basket, with interstices closed with soaproot gelatine, and the handled seed beater, were the usual utensils used in gathering. Sifting, winnowing, and pulverizing in the bedrock mortar followed. Parching took place in many cases before pulverizing, and consisted of shaking the seeds in a shallow parching basket with live coals. The natural oil in some seeds made the forming of meal cakes, cones, and balls an easy matter. Seed meal was regarded as particularly fine eating. Visitors were given it to eat along with their acorn mush, which was regarded as insipid without such accompaniment.

Many bulbs, corms, tubers, and roots were eaten. These are now commonly referred to as "Indian potatoes." They were secured with the digging stick, and were preferably baked or steamed in the earth oven, or roasted in the ashes of the open fire, or, if the quantity was small, stone-boiled in baskets. When roasted, the ashes were sifted from them by means of an ordinary winnowing basket. "Indian potatoes" were also dried for winter use, first being oven baked. They were stored in baskets in the dwelling, never in a cache as were acorns. Sometimes the stored ones were pulverized and cooked as mush or porridge.

Several fungi were eaten, but only a puff ball has been identified. They were gathered by both men and women. Mushrooms were gathered in April and May, puff balls in the summer and fall. Mushrooms in general were called helli (C), also the name of one species. Shredded and dried mushrooms were boiled and eaten with salt, or were ground in a mortar and cooked as soup.

Greens were usually eaten after boiling. The surplus was steamed in the earth oven, dried, and stored for winter use. When needed it

---

[10]Jepson, 1921, 243.

was soaked in cold water and either boiled again or eaten without further cooking. Water cress is eaten now, but is said to have been introduced by Chinese in the mining days of the nineteenth century.

Many plants were used medicinally.

OAKS AND ACORNS

Of the many vegetable foods used, acorns (muyu) were the staple. The nuts kept for months and were stored whole in outdoor granaries called tca'kka (P, N, C, S), or in small quantities in baskets indoors. Oak flowers are called hesaka (C); oak leaves, takta (C); oak balls, amayaka (C); oak gall balls, hopoto (C)-literally "spherical"; and oak leaf raspberry galls, yotcito (C).

The following are the oaks mentioned by Miwok informants:

California Black Oak (*Quercus kelloggii* Newb.), telē'lĭ (P, N), tele'lĭ (C), te'lelĭ (S).

White, or Valley, Oak (*Quercus lobata* Neé), sī'wek (P), mo'lla (N, C), lē'ka (C).

Interior Live Oak (*Quercus wislizenii* A.DC.), sa'sa (P, N), sako'sa (C), sakasa (C).

Large scrub oak (*Quercus wislizenii* A.DC.), sasa (C).

Water, Blue, Swamp, or Post Oak (*Quercus douglasii* H. & A.), ala'wa (P, N), otca'pa (P), wilisu (C).

Small bushy scrub oak (*Quercus sp.*), sakwuba (C). Evergreen.

Bushy little oak (*Quercus sp.*), hakine (C).

The Central Miwok of the Transition zone grade acorns in the following order: teleli, sakasa, leka, sasa (yellow meat), hakine, sakwuba, wilisu. The poorest (wilisu) were so graded because the soup (nüppa) made from them was watery and the bread or biscuits fell to pieces. Although white oak acorns make excellent food, they are placed second in the list, because of difficulty in hulling. When held on end on a stone anvil and struck with a hammerstone like other acorns, the hulls do not crack open readily but have a tendency to mash. For this reason they were usually hulled with the teeth. In 1922 one aged informant was forced to use these acorns, because of shortage of black oak acorns. The hammerstone crushed them too much and her few remaining teeth were inadequate, so she peeled them with a steel pocket knife.

In the open valley of the Plains area the principal oak was the water oak. Its acorns were gathered in great quantities and some were traded to the hill dwellers for other foods, including different species of acorns. Fish were similarly traded by the valley people.

Acorns were gathered in burden baskets, plate LIV, when they fell from the trees in the late autumn and early winter. Especially in times of shortage, the trees, in which the California woodpecker had drilled holes and stored acorns, were examined and the fresh acorns pried out with a pointed instrument (welup, N) of deer antler (kī'lī, N). See plate LVIII, fig. 11.)

The acorn anvil was called ülü'we (P), ü'mme (N), tū'ka (C), mū'laa (S). The hammerstone, a natural pebble, plate XXXII, fig. 6, was called lū'pû (P), lū'pu (N), lū'ppu (C), and pasa'kkila (S), Sometimes an unworked flat stone (never steatite) was used as the anvil, but frequently a special stone with several small, pecked, cuppings was employed. Sometimes the portable mortar, provided with one or more small cuppings on its underside, was upturned and used for the purpose. The shucks, called müyü (N), and moʈo'kkī (C), were discarded, or sometimes burned as they made a very hot and lasting fire. The plump meats (katü'ma N, and kaʈumu C), were placed in a basket and later ground into meal, called telē'lī (N), ka'wannû (C), usually on the bedrock mortar, plate XXIX, fig. 2, but sometimes in the movable mortar, plate XXXIV. The bedrock mortars were merely large flat out-croppings of the bedrock of the region. Such a surface might contain from one to perhaps a couple of dozen of the cuppings or mortar holes, depending upon the population and age of a village. These cuppings were abandoned after they had worn to a depth of perhaps five inches. Such a bedrock mortar was a community "mill" and here at times the women congregated in numbers to do their grinding and to chat. Sometimes one of these bedrock mortars was protected from the weather by means of a small conical slab house such as that shown in plate XXX, fig. 2, which shows also seven of the cobblestone pestles which were found in this same house.

A peck or two of shelled acorn meats were placed on the mortar and the woman sat with her legs spread out straight on either side of the grinding area. The cobblestone pestle (plate XXXIII, fig. 1-6) was grasped in both hands and raised to about eye level. The body, hinging at the waist, swung backward as the pestle was raised and forward as it descended. As the grinding progressed and the acorns were reduced to coarse meal, it was kept in a ring, a foot or two in diameter and four or five inches high, with a crater in its center directly over the cupping in the mortar. The jar of the pounding shook down, both inside and outside the crater, the coarser particles of meal. Those in the crater fell automatically under the next blow of the pestle. At intervals of fifteen or twenty strokes of the pestle those coarse particles on the outside were scraped up with the hands and over into the crater. This process continued, with occasionally a general sweeping up with the soaproot brush (plate XXXVI), until the whole mass was reduced to a relatively fine meal. This was sifted repeatedly and the coarser meal (wassa'yû, C) returned for further grinding. Holmes[11] describes and illustrates the process. He observed the woman scrape up the large particles with one hand after each blow of the pestle.

Informants maintained that originally the sifting was done only with the closely coiled, discoidal basket, plate XLIX, fig. 4 and 5, called tū'ma. Later the flat, finely twined, triangular basket[12] was introduced from the Washo and Paiute country and was as much used as the original Miwok form.

The sifting basket was held at an angle of about forty-five degrees toward the worker. It was gently shaken up and down, the upper edge moving somewhat more than the lower, until all the finer meal formed a solid mass adhering to the basket. This motion at the same time brought the coarser particles to the surface and caused them to roll down and off the edge of the basket. When no more coarse particles would roll off, two or three fingers were run through the meal to loosen it from the basket, and the whole process was repeated. After three or four such siftings, no more coarse meal remained in the basket, and the fine meal was poured into another basket as finished. When finely ground, such meal stuck quite firmly to the basket. It was loosened by a couple of sound taps with the tips of the fingers on any conveniently exposed portion of the basket. Finally, the basket was thoroughly brushed with the soaproot brush. Sifting was done on a still day if possible, as the wind tended to blow away the fine meal.

The pulverized root of *Peltiphyllum peltatum* (Torr.) Engler. (senseteko, C) was sometimes mixed with acorn meal to whiten it. The green leaves of Spanish Clover (*Lotus americanus* [Nutt.] Bisch.) (pulluluku, C) were pounded with acorns that were too oily, to absorb some of the oil. They did not alter the flavor of the acorn meal. A

---

[11]Anthropological Studies in California.
[12]Cf. Gifford, 1932, pl. 5.

third plant which was at times pulverized and mixed with acorn meal intended for "bread" making was the root of either a pond lily or a cattail.

The tannin in the acorns made it impossible to use the meal directly from the mortar. It must first be leached. When possible a sandy spot was chosen and a shallow basin, three or four feet in diameter, was scooped out. In this the meal was placed and water was poured over it. As the water soaked through the fine meal it dissolved out the acid and leached it down through the porous sand. In order to leach the meal evenly it was necessary to distribute the water equally over the whole surface. Therefore, after the meal was first thoroughly wet, small radial furrows were made, usually with the fingers, to conduct the water from the center to all parts.

Lacking a natural sandy spot, an artificial one was constructed, like that shown in the background in plate XXX, fig. 1. Usually in the shadow of the brush sunshade, such a pit was made by first putting down a layer of boughs in the form of the required basin. This was then lined with fine grass to keep the sand from running through. Upon this was placed an inch or two of sand. Both types of leaching pit were called mo'lappa (N, S), molpa (C).

To break the fall of the water on the surface of the meal a small bundle of green conifer twigs was used. Douglas fir (tcapaha, C), white fir (tuttukine, C), incense cedar (mō'nōku, N, C, S), and tamarack (katabi, C) were thus used. The leaves were put over the meal in the leaching basin, or held in the hand, to break the force of the water and to cause it to spread, instead of striking the meal as a single stream. The first two or three applications of water were cold. Then lukewarm water was used. Each application thereafter was a few degrees warmer, until quite hot water was used. Usually ten applications of water sufficed to remove the tannin. The meal was tested, not only by tasting, but by running the finger through it to the bottom of the basin in several places and observing its color, which was whitish, rather than yellow or brown, if the leaching was complete. Leached acorn meal was called hutayu (C).

The leached meal was removed by placing the hand palm downward, spread to its fullest extent, on the meal, which adhered to the hand and clove easily from the sandy basin. The sand which adhered was easily removed by pouring water over it. The small amount of meal which was washed away with the sand was recovered by decanting the water from it, after it had settled in the basket used to catch the water, which was poured repeatedly over the successive handfuls of meal.

When a small amount of meal was to be leached it was sometimes done in a coarsely woven, triangular sifting basket. The basket was lined with a layer of leaves of *Lupinus latifolius* Agardh., to prevent the meal running through the interstices. The meal was placed on these leaves and leached as in the leaching pit.

The leached meal was cooked as soup, mush, "biscuits," or "bread." "Soup" was a thin gruel (nü'ppa, P, N, C, S). "Mush" was cooked to a thick glutenous state by adding a greater amount of meal to a given quantity of water. It was called yo'kko (P, N), and was eaten by dipping with the first and second fingers. The shell of a freshwater mussel (sopo'nūī, C) was also used as a spoon (a'tkal, P; a'tkalu, N; talī'pa, C).

The typical mush stirrer of the north is a wooden paddle (plate XXXI, figs. 1-4), that of the south a looped stick (plate XXXI, fig. 5). In the Central Miwok region the two types overlap. Occasionally a paddle has a slight dish or curve to the blade to facilitate the removal of hot stones (hoñoya, C) from cooking baskets. The paddles were made of oak (*Quercus*) in several cases and of manzanita (*Arctostaphylos*) in one case. At least two of four looped mush stirrers noted are of oak. A young black oak branch was preferred. The looped stirrers have two string bindings; one at the base, the other near the end, of the handle.

The principal steps of the acorn industry are admirably illustrated by Holmes[13] for the Central Miwok at Murphys, Calaveras county. In his plate 11 Holmes shows the use of the metate and muller. Our informants did not mention their use in the acorn industry, and moreover said that any use of them was a modern innovation from east of the Sierra Nevada. If this is so, then the Miwok have adapted it to the preparation of acorn meal, for which it is not used in the Great Basin, as oaks are absent from that region.

The usual form of biscuit, ūlē' (P, N), u'le (C. of mts., S), and mosakala (C of hills), was made of acorn mush, cooked somewhat longer, and often further thickened by "dipping" it with a small dipper basket (plate XLV, figs. 1 and 2). It was dipped up and poured

---

[13]Holmes, 1902, pls. 10-15.

slowly, from a height of perhaps two feet, back into the cooking basket. The effect is not certain, but informants maintained that it thickened the mush and rendered it more gelatinous. When the proper consistency had been attained the mush was dipped out in this same small basket, which was placed for a minute or two in cold water, preferably a pool in a running stream. As the basket cooled its contents loosened easily from its surface and by deftly overturning the basket a small loaf of "bread" was slid out into the water. Here it remained until thoroughly cooled, when it had about the consistency of a modern gelatine dessert. If not cooled internally it was apt to go to pieces when handled. It was an excellent daily food and also found much use at feasts.

In cooking all three of these acorn products, soup, mush, and biscuits, boiling with hot stones was the universal method. Often steatite stones were employed. The water was placed in a large (about 30 quarts capacity) cooking basket, set in a pit two or three inches deep to guard against capsizing. About a dozen hot cooking stones, tū'le (N) (plate XXXII, figs. 1-4), were placed in the basket by means of a pair of long, wooden tongs, ta'lapa (N), pīnīra (C) (plate XXXI, figs. 6 and 7), used as illustrated in plate XXX, fig. 1. Each stone was first dipped in a basket of water to cleanse it. Meanwhile about two quarts of the newly leached meal were thoroughly mixed by the hands in a small basket with six or seven quarts of warm water from the big boiling basket. Except for a small amount, this was poured into another large basket. Hot stones were put into this thin gruel until it boiled violently and cooked thoroughly. As the cooking progressed more water or more gruel was added, to attain the desired consistency.

When placed in the basket the cooking stones were at almost white heat. They were prevented from burning the basket by constant stirring with a paddle (plate XXXI, figs. 1-4), called sa'lakka (P), tcawa'lli and tōlō'wa (N), uta'wa (C), and tolō'wa (S), which was also used, among the Northern Miwok, to dip out the stones. A looped stirrer (sawa'iya, C, S), (plate XXXI, fig. 5), was used among the Central and Southern Miwok for this purpose.

A small basket with about two quarts of cold water was placed against the cooking basket. As the stones were lifted out of the latter the mush was scraped off with the fingers, and the stones dropped into the basket of cold water. Any adherent mush congealed and, when the stones cooled, was easily peeled off. More or less broke off or accumulated in the bottom of the basket. The water was drained off and this was eaten, or when the stones had been washed for the last time, the contents of this washing basket were poured into the cooking basket and the whole stirred to an even consistency. These salvaged particles of mush were called tcunupati (C). The process of boiling resulted in ten to twelve quarts of acorn soup, or a somewhat smaller amount of the thicker mush, from the original two quarts of meal.

Two kinds of bread, "leavened" or black, and "unleavened" or white, were baked in the earth oven. These were called respectively hū'iтcu (P), pū'lla (N); and ūta'ya (P, N), yo'ko (N). The "leavened" bread was dark brown in color, and was made of the acorns of the "water" oak, ala'wa (P, N). The "leavening" was a small quantity of ashes of water oak bark added to the dough. This sweetened the bread decidedly, though it did not make it rise.

Among the Central Miwok the word pulla applies to a bread made directly from freshly leached acorn meal baked on a hot stone. It is turned as it is cooked, until finally brown.

THE BUCKEYE

The buckeye (*Æsculus californica* [Spach.] Nutt.) tree and its nuts were called unu (P, N) and siwü (C). In times of scarcity the nuts were eaten. The process of preparation was tedious because of the protracted leaching. The resulting product was a soup (nüppa, C). The nuts were collected after they had fallen to the ground, in the autumn. They were roasted in hot ashes, or sometimes boiled, and then peeled, the cover being broken with the teeth. The meats were mashed in the hands in a basket of water. The fine particles settled to the bottom. When there was a sufficient accumulation it was poured into a winnowing basket, set over a large, deep basket. The fine particles ran through the interstices of the winnowing basket with the water. The coarser pieces were retained in the winnowing basket, which was then set in running water, where it remained eighteen hours or more. It was then ready to eat without further cooking.

The fine meal was put in a leaching basin, excavated in the ground. It was leached with cold water, a process which took about eighteen hours, often from noon until the following morning. Thereafter it was ready to eat. No lining was put in the leaching basin. The meal rested right against the sand. Night work by torch light was necessitated by the lengthy period of the leaching. It was done by women. When the leaching was completed, the meal was taken up with the hands and placed in a large basket. No further cooking was necessary. In partaking of the meal, it was mixed with water in a small basket and drunk.

Unroasted buckeye nuts were stored for long periods and sometimes remained edible until the next fall, when the acorn crop was ripe. The eating of buckeye nuts was resorted to only when the acorn crop failed.

CONIFERS

A number of generic terms for parts of conifers were used. Sowi (C) is the term for cones, sakku (C) denotes nuts, also those of other plants. Perhaps this is a term originally applied to the digger pine nuts and later extended to all nuts. Thus, soloku sakku is hazel nut. Yutu (C) is the pitch, sakuta (C) the gum, hose (C) the needles, semmila (C) the bark, of pines; ene'na (N, C, S) the bark of the incense cedar (*Libocedrus decurrens* Torr.), mō'nōku (N, C, S). The gum was usually found near the base of a tree, especially one which had been burnt. It was chewed, particularly by young people. Gum of the western yellow pine was specifically mentioned.

A heavy smudge of pine needles was applied to the wound of a person bitten by a black spider. Anyone might do this for the patient.

The two pines largely sought for edible nuts were the Digger Pine (*Pinus sabiniana* Dougl.) of the Upper Sonoran foothills and the Sugar Pine (*Pinus lambertiana* Dougl.) of the Transition mountains.

DIGGER PINE (*Pinus sabiniana* Dougl.). Sa'kkü (P), ca'kü (P, N), sa'kü (N), ka'wil (N), sakku (C), sa'kü (N, S). The Digger Pine is the characteristic pine of the Upper Sonoran zone and its blue-green needles make it conspicuous.

The nuts and the pith of the cones were eaten, the needles used for thatch, bedding, and floor covering; the bark for house covering, the twigs and rootlets as sewing material for coiled basket, and charcoal from the nut meats was crushed in the hand and applied to sores, burns, and abrasions. In spring the green cones were collected for nuts and pith. The cones could not be knocked off with sticks, but had to be twisted off by hand. Men usually climbed for them. The green cones were beaten with a stone until the covering split, when it was easily peeled off. The nuts were soft-shelled at this stage and shell as well as meat was eaten. Green cones and soft-shelled nuts were called ellati (C). The pithy center of the green cone is called tcuku (C). It was roasted some twenty minutes in hot ashes, yielding a brownish, pithy, sweetish food, to a slight extent syrupy.

The fully mature brown cones and nuts fallen to the ground are called lippasi (C). They attain maturity in September. The nuts were stored in hupulu coiled baskets. The cones were placed in a fire long enough to burn off adherent pitch, so as to facilitate handling. The cone was then split open with a stone and torn to pieces to extract the nuts. These were sometimes eaten raw, but were usually parched with live coals in the flat parching and sifting basket.

WESTERN YELLOW PINE (*Pinus ponderosa* Dougl.). This common pine of the Miwok mountain country is called wa'ssa (C). Because of the smallness of the nuts the natives seldom gathered the cones either green or ripe. When gathered they were dried in the sun to extract the nuts.

SUGAR PINE (*Pinus lambertiana* Dougl.). Caña'kū or sa'ñagu (N) and hi'ñatcī (C) are the terms for both old and young sugar pine trees. This species, like the digger pine, supplied a much relished nut. The cones were not twisted off by hand, but by imparting to the limb to which they were attached first a swaying, then a rotating, motion which caused the heavy cones to twist themselves off. In order to do this it was necessary for men to climb the tree and use the hand or foot to get the branch into motion. This was done when the cone had turned brown, but just before it was mature enough for the nuts to fall out. Green cones were not gathered. If a tree presented a great expanse of smooth trunk, a small dead tree was set against it to serve as a ladder (tcone, C), or a special climbing pole (aña, C) was used. Smaller trees were scaled without any type of ladder.

After the sugar pine cones were all shaken down, as much as half a ton had been accumulated in some cases. They were collected by the women and stood together upside down, sometimes in two tiers. Dry pine needles were then spread over them and ignited, to burn off the pitch, a process called hiñatci mulu (C). Sugar pine needles were used for no other purpose.

The sugar pine cones were next hammered top down on a rock so that they split down the middle. The nuts were then removed by pressing down each projecting point on the cone so that the nut would roll out. The nuts were still warm and some might be eaten at once, although pressing and blowing of the eater by a shaman was regarded as necessary at first, as with most first fruits among the Miwok.

The nuts were next shaken in a winnowing basket to get rid of any chaff or empty shells. The wind was the draft of air that removed the waste.

As a rule the man who climbed the tree divided the nuts among the men and women of his party.

In addition to shelling the nuts, which are soft shelled, and eating the meat whole, the Central Miwok pulverized the nuts, shell as well as meat, in a mortar until they had the consistency of peanut butter, but a darker color. This sugar pine nut butter was called lopa (C), a generic term for all such preparations. Sugar pine nuts were prepared as lopa especially for feasts (kote, C). Digger pine nuts could not be prepared as lopa, because their shells are too hard and thick. Sugar pine lopa was eaten with the fingers along with acorn soup (nüppa, C), or with manzanita cider (sakema, C).

Sugar pine sugar was dissolved and used as a wash for sore or blind eyes. It was also eaten as a delicacy.

SIERRA JUNIPER (*Juniperus occidentalis* Hook.). What an informant said was juniper is the tree called setekine (C). The nuts were eaten when thoroughly ripe. The several nuts in each cone were cracked with the teeth and eaten without further preparation. The nuts seem to have been less troublesome to get than pine nuts, because of the lack of pitch. The tree produced no gum. Aside from the seeds no parts of the tree were used.

SEEDS

Wissler has designated California and adjacent regions as the wild seed area.[14] The Miwok are true to type in this respect, as wild seeds, including acorns and buckeyes, are their dietary mainstay. Most wild seeds are eaten in the form of pinole, or meal, produced by pulverizing the seeds in a mortar. The metate was not employed for this purpose

---

[14] Wissler, fig. 1.

by the Miwok, except as an allegedly intrusive modern implement from the Great Basin.

The following discussion concerns seeds and nuts other than the acorns and buckeye. None required leaching. Most all were winnowed to remove chaff, parched with coals in a basket, and pulverized. Most were eaten in the form of dry meal, others were mixed with water, and some were cooked as a mush or porridge.

The seventeen identified species are listed in alphabetic order. Only three used by the Miwok were used by the Yuki and Pomo, although in three cases different species of the same genus were used by these peoples: *Boisduvalia densiflora*[15] (Lindl.) Wats., *Corylus rostrata* Ait. *californica*[16] A.DC., *Madia dissitiflora* (Nutt.) T. & G.[17]

OATS (*Avena barbata* Brot.). Aweni (C), obviously a corruption of Spanish avena. When ripe the seeds were gathered with a seed-beater and carrying basket. They were pounded lightly in a mortar merely to loosen the husks, not to pulverize the seeds. Then followed winnowing. After that the seeds were parched with coals in a parching basket. The seeds were next pulverized in a mortar, and finally stone-boiled in a basket, making a soup or mush called tcista (C).

BALSAM ROOT (*Balsamorrhiza sagittata* Nutt.). Ho'tcõtca (C). The seeds were cracked with mortar and pestle, winnowed, and eaten.

DENSE-FLOWERED EVENING PRIMROSE (*Boisduvalia densiflora* [Lindl.] Wats.). Winiwayu (C), wawõ'na (S). The seeds were gathered with a seed-beater and burden basket, parched, pulverized, and eaten dry. Those stored were unparched.

UPRIGHT EVENING PRIMROSE (*Boisduvalia stricta* [Gray] Greene). Winiwayu (C). The seeds were gathered with the seed-beater in the fall. They were parched and pulverized, and the meal eaten dry.

"RIPGUT" GRASS (*Bromus rigidus* Roth., var. *gussonei* [Parl] Coss. & Dur.). Sü'llü (C). The seeds were pulverized and eaten as pinole.

RED MAIDS (*Calandrinia caulescens* H. B. K. var.*menziesii*, Gray). The prized seed from this small plant was called ko'tca (N, C). These black seeds were very rich and oily and were eaten pulverized. About

---

[15]Chesnut, 370.
[16]Chesnut, 333.
[17]Chesnut, 395.

the end of May the entire plants were pulled up and spread out on cleanly swept hard ground, or on a granite outcrop, to dry. With drying the seeds tended to separate, and by striking the drying plants the separation was accelerated. Lastly the plants were picked up and shaken to get additional seeds. Thereafter they were thrown away.

The seeds were then swept together with a soaproot brush and placed in a very tight, coiled, flat-bottomed basket. The winnowing was with the aid of the wind and was done in a tight winnowing basket (hetalu, C), different from the openwork winnower (tcamayu, C). Then followed thorough drying and storage in a flat-bottomed coiled hupulu basket.

In preparing kotca seed as food a quantity was parched in a discoidal basket plate (kewayu, C) about four inches deep. The mass of seeds and coals was turned over with a rotary motion by skillful manipulation of the basket. After parching, the seeds were pulverized with a stone pestle in a bedrock mortar. The meal was very oily and was pressed into balls and cakes for eating.

PAINTED CUP (*Castilleia sp.*). Ponko (C). Gathered in June with seed-beater. Dried and stored for winter. Parched, pounded, eaten dry.

FITCH'S SPIKEWEED (*Centromadia fitchii* [Gray] Greene). Its seeds were eaten in the form of mush.

CLARKIA (*Clarkia elegans* Dougl.). Sokowila (C). The seeds were collected in a finely woven burden basket (tcikali, C) with the aid of a seed-beater. After drying they were parched and pulverized in a mortar. The meal was eaten dry with acorn mush. Sometimes the whole plant was dried and the seeds removed later.

HAZEL (*Corylus rostrata* Ait. var. *californica* A. DC.). So'lōkō, so'llogū (N); mūla', so'lokū, li'ma (C); mü'la (S). The nuts were used to a limited extent as food.

SUMMER'S DARLING (*Godetia amoena* [Lehm.] Lilja.). Sipsibe (C), The whole plant was pulled up and dried as soon as the flowering was over. With the drying the seeds popped out. These were parched, pulverized, and eaten dry.

FAREWELL TO SPRING (*Godetia biloba* [Dur.] Wats.). Witala (C). The seeds of this plant were gathered in June. The tops of the plants were broken off and tied in large bundles, using the stem of one for binding. They were then dried on a granite outcrop, without untying the bundles. The hot summer sun prevented molding. When thoroughly dry the bundles were opened and spread. Treading and beating with sticks loosened the seeds, which were gathered and then winnowed in the wind. The cleaned seeds were then stored in a hupulu basket. They were parched and pulverized before eating.

FAREWELL TO SPRING (*Godetia viminea* Spach.). Nuwati, nō'watcī, nō'wasī (C). The entire plants were pulled up, bound in sheaves, placed in water for two hours, and laid on a granite outcrop to dry. The pods opened, releasing the seeds. This process was facilitated by beating the bundles with a stick. The seeds were winnowed and stored. In preparing them for food they were pulverized, but were eaten dry and uncooked.

GUM-WEED (*Madia dissitiflora* [Nutt.] T. & G.). Etce' (C). The seeds of this tarweed were among the most valued. They were harvested in August with the aid of the seed-beater, winnowed, and stored in baskets. The method of preparation was to parch with coals in a parching basket, rewinnow, and lastly to pulverize in a mortar. The resulting meal was oily and could be readily picked up in lumps.

TARWEED (*Madia elegans* Don.). Yō'wa (C, S). Its seeds were gathered in midsummer, being struck off with the seed-beater into a soaproot-lined burden basket (waka, C). Yowa seeds were harvested by women during a period of a fortnight. They were easily kept in storage and sometimes the supply lasted a year, until the next harvest.

The seeds were winnowed, the husks or chaff (pusela, C)[18] being blown away by the wind. The seeds were pulverized in a bedrock mortar with a stone pestle, being ground very fine. Both winnowing and sifting (pika, to sift, in C) were done in a flat circular basket plaque (hetalu, C). The sifting was done by jiggling the plaque so that the big fragments separated from the fine meal. The large fragments were pulverized further. The meal was eaten dry.

CHILE TARWEED (*Madia sativa* Molina.). The seeds are used as food.

---

[18]Cf. puselu, to blow; puse, to winnow.

BUENA MUJER (*Mentzelia sp.*). Matcū' (C). The seeds were pulverized and eaten as pinole.

SKUNKWEED (*Navarretia sp.*). Hañu (C). Gathered with seed-beater in August, sun dried, stored. Parched and pulverized. Eaten dry.

VALLEY TASSELS (*Orthocarpus attenuatus* Gray). Tummu (C). The seed was gathered with the seed-beater and burden basket, dried, parched, and pulverized. It was eaten dry.

CALIFORNIA BUTTERCUP (*Ranunculus californicus* Benth.). Takalu (C). The seeds were gathered in June with the seed-beater and soap-root-lined burden basket. The processes involved in order, were winnowing in the wind, drying, storing; and, when eaten, parching and pulverizing in a bedrock mortar.

Unidentified seeds which were eaten are hetchetci (C), a grass growing in Hetch Hetchy valley and from which a mush was made; ho'tcōta (C); ka'llu (C), flat, curved, black seeds from which a meal was made; mūkū'sū (S); o'pkole (S); oppole (C); po'sowila (C), plant flowers in June; pū'ka (C); sitila (N), flattish seed from a meadow plant which grows a foot high, burned as offerings; siya (C); sulle (C); talaku (C); tca'nта (S), grows at higher altitude than Miwok habitat, meal boiled and drunk as a gruel; tokobu (N), a globular seed from a single-stemmed, two-foot high plant with pale blue flowers, seeds explode with noise when burned; üsüka (C); yū'та (C), flat, curved, brown seeds.

BULBS AND CORMS

Bulbs and corms, vernacularly "wild potatoes," were important in the Miwok dietary. The names of twenty-eight were recorded, but only twelve of these have been identified, and one of these, the snake lily (*Brodiaea volubilis* [Kell.] Baker), was not eaten. Of the twelve identified two are used by the Yuki and Pomo: White Mariposa lily (*Calochortus venustus*[19] Dougl.) and *Carum kelloggii*[20] Gray. The root fibers of the latter are also used for brushes, a use quite unknown to the Miwok.

[19]Chesnut, 323.
[20]Chesnut, 372.

OOKOW (*Brodiaea pulchella* [Salisb.] Greene). Silüwü (C). Steamed in the earth oven and eaten in the same fashion as *Brodiaea coronaria*.

HARVEST BRODIAEA (*Brodiaea coronaria* [Salisb.] Jepson). Walla (C). It is dug about the first of May when its shoots are just appearing above ground. The bulb lies deeper in the ground than that of the Mariposa lily. It was dug by both men and women, the occasion being a four-day excursion and picnic. The time for the digging was set by the chief. Four days were spent in digging the bulbs, during which time none was eaten. The bulbs were transported in burden baskets to the cooking place, where they were cooked in the earth oven on the fourth day.

The earth oven for the bulbs consisted of a hole about a foot or foot and a half deep and three feet in diameter, excavated with the digging stick. Stones were heated in a fire built beside the pit. When the fire had burnt down the coals were raked into the pit and the hot stones put on top of them. Over the stones were put the broad leaves of the *Wyethia helenioides* Nutt. When the stones were completely covered by the leaves, the bulbs were poured into the pit to a depth of about six inches. These bulbs were covered with leaves, on which hot stones were placed. The whole was covered with earth. Then water was poured around the edges of the pit, so that it worked down to the hot stones and coals, thus producing steam for the cooking which lasted about one hour. After cooking, the bulbs were removed by hand and placed in an openwork basket tray (tcamayu, C). Then a second and a third lot were cooked if the quantity gathered was large. Both walla and Mariposa lily bulbs were eaten without salt.

WHITE BRODIAEA (*Brodiaea hyacinthina* [Lindl.] Baker). Wüsumayü (C). The bulbs were dug from a depth of several inches at the same season as *B. coronaria* and *Calochortus venustus*. They were steamed in the earth oven with *B. coronaria*.

GOLDEN BRODIAEA (*Brodiaea ixioides* [Ait.f] Wats.). Silüwü (C). The bulbs were eaten.

"NIGGER-TOE" (*Brodiaea sp.*). Tene (C). Cooked and eaten.

GRASS NUTS (*Brodiaea sp.*). Wata' (C). Eaten.

WHITE MARIPOSA LILY (*Calochortus venustus* Dougl.). Tcikimtci (C). The bulbs were usually dug when buds appeared on the plant in April. However, they could be dug much later as long as the flower marked the spot. The bulbs were usually about six inches deep and were dug with the digging stick by both men and women. The bulbs keep only four or five days, then shrivel. Therefore, they cannot be stored for later use. The bulbs were roasted for about twenty minutes in the ashes of a fire that had died down. When extracted they were soft, like boiled potatoes. No ceremony was necessary before the eating of the first of the crop of this bulb, except for dancers who always had to be pressed before eating the first of any new food. Sometimes the Mariposa lily bulbs were cooked in the earth oven with the bulbs of *Brodiaea coronaria*. Yellow Mariposa lilies (*Calochortus luteus* Dougl.) are called tcikimtci susa (C) and the bulbs are prepared and eaten like those of the white variety.

SQUAW-ROOT (*Carum gairdneri* Gray). Tuñi (C), siketi (C), ᴛu'ñi (S). Boiled and eaten like a potato. Its meat is white.

ANISE (*Carum kelloggii* Gray). Sakasu (C), sa'kkasu (S). Eaten.

SOAPROOT (*Chlorogalum pomeridianum* [Ker] Kunth.). A small mild soaproot (so'pa, P; sôpa, N) was eaten. It was wilted and rubbed to remove the dried outer leaf parts. Baking in the earth oven followed. The bulbs were also dried without baking for winter use. Soaking was then necessary before baking. The uses of this plant for fish poison, for detergent, for glue, and for brushes are discussed elsewhere.

EULOPHUS (*Eulophus bolanderi* [Gray] C. & R.) Olasi (C). Cooked in baskets by stone-boiling for ten minutes, becoming mealy like potatoes. They were then peeled and eaten. When the acorn supply was much reduced or exhausted, as in June, they served as a substitute. When so used, they were washed, sun-dried three or four days with skin on, and pounded in a bedrock mortar. The resulting meal was cooked in a basket to form siwüla (C), the equivalent of nüppa or acorn soup. Although pounded with skin on, *Eulophus bolanderi* yielded a white meal. The soup or mush prepared therefrom was also made into biscuits (ule, C). *Eulophus bolanderi* was quite palatable raw as well as cooked. It was preserved by mashing, drying, and basket storing. When needed it was repulverized and cooked. Pressing, blowing, and sucking of prospective eaters were performed for the first of the crop, which was gathered at the behest of the chief. The officiant pretended to suck a bulb from each person's forehead. This followed the division of the olasi by the chief to the different families. Olasi bulbs are said to grow particularly well on lava beds; for example, near Strawberry, Tuolumne county.

St. John's Wort (*Hypericum formosum*, H. B. K. var. *scouleri* Coulter). A'iisa (C). Eaten fresh as it came from the ground, or dried, ground into flour, and used like acorn meal.

Corn Lily (*Veratrum californicum* Durand). Sulumta (C). Roasted in hot ashes, peeled, and eaten. It was not stored.

Unidentified bulbs and corms were the following: keleme (C); lippasi (C), stem eaten; o'llūtcū (S), very sweet; popkine (C), stem eaten; pū'kpūkū (S); seladi (C); siksile (C), prepared like *Eulophus bolanderi*, when eaten raw having a flavor like parsnips, which disappeared with cooking; solasi (C), stem eaten; tcikiwitci (C), white meat, boiled; tcīтī'ksa (S); tipi (C), not eaten, because sickening; тū'lla (S), grows near stream banks, pulverized and cooked as porridge like acorn meal; тūsū'mkele (C), roasted in hot ashes about five minutes; yumutu (C), a long bulb or corm, boiled; yûtcotu (C).

GREENS

The number of species of plants eaten as greens outnumbered those used in the modern dietary. Thirty-seven species were recorded, of which twenty-one have been identified. Most greens were eaten after stone-boiling in a basket or after steaming in the earth oven. Some were eaten raw. They were usually eaten as accompaniment to acorn soup.

Of the species used by the Miwok, the following were recorded among the Pomo and Yuki: *Asclepias mexicana*[21] Cav., flowers eaten; *Chenopodium album*[22] L., leaves eaten; *Delphinium hesperium*[23] Gray, not used; *Mimulus guttatus*[24] DC., leaves eaten; *Trifolium ciliatum*[25] Nutt., leaves eaten sparingly.

---

[21]Chesnut, 380.
[22]Chesnut, 346.
[23]Chesnut, 347.
[24]Chesnut, 387.
[25]Chesnut, 360.

The following list gives the botanical name, the Miwok name, the manner of preparation, and any additional notes of interest.

COLUMBINE (*Aquilegia truncata* (F. & M). Tcuyuma (C). Boiled. Early spring.

MILKWEED (*Asclepias mexicana* Cav.). Istawü (C). Boiled, but goes to pieces. Sometimes the boiled material was added to manzanita cider to thicken it.

WHITE GOOSEFOOT (*Chenopodium album* L.,). Somala (C). Boiled. Sometimes dried and stored for later use.

WESTERN LARKSPUR (*Delphinium hesperium* Gray). Kowe (C). Leaves and flowers boiled.

LARKSPUR (*Delphinium sp.*). Witilima (C). Boiled in March when young.

HORSEWEED (*Erigeron canadensis* L.). Mututa (C). Leaves and tender tops pounded in the bedrock mortar. Eaten pulverized, but uncooked. Flavor like onions.

TIBINAGUA (*Eriogonum nudum* Dougl.). Sapü'la, sapasu (C). Eaten raw. Sour flavor.

ALUM ROOT (*Heuchera micrantha* Dougl.) Tcuyuma (C). Leaves first to be eaten in spring. Boiled or steamed. After steaming a certain quantity might be dried and stored.

WILD PEA (*Lathyrus vestitus* Nutt.). Lulumati (C), lu'lumet (S). Eaten as greens. Seeds eaten raw.

ROSE LUPINE (*Lupinus densiflorus* Benth.), tūlmī'ssa (C). Early in the spring its leaves and flowers, stripped from the stalk by running the hand along it, were steamed in the earth oven, and eaten with acorn soup (nüppa, C). This plant was regarded as common daily food for which no pressing and blowing ceremony was required. A white variety called tokola (C) was also used.

BROAD-LEAVED LUPINE (*Lupinus latifolius* Agardh.). Wataksa (C), wa'taksa (S), tcī'ūtcīūwa (C). Its leaves and flowers were also steamed in the earth oven and were preferred to *L. densiflorus*. After steaming, quantities were dried and stored for winter use, being placed in large hupulu baskets. When eaten in the winter, the dried leaves and flowers were usually boiled, after soaking in cold water three or four hours to remove the bitter taste. Sometimes they were eaten without further boiling and served as a relish with manzanita cider.

COMMON MONKEY FLOWER (*Mimulus guttatus* DC.). Puksa (C). The leaves were boiled.

MUSK-PLANT (*Mimulus moschatus* Dougl.). Pokosa, yusunu (C). When young this plant was boiled. It was not stored for winter use, because the quantity obtainable was always small.

MINER'S LETTUCE (*Montia perfoliata* [Donn.] Howell). Sestu (C). The stems, leaves, and blossoms of this plant were eaten raw.

TWIGGY WATER DROPWORT (*Œnanthe sp.*). Komani (C). Stems eaten raw.

SWEET CICELY (*Osmorrhiza nuda* Torr.). Tcuyuma (C). The leaves were boiled.

SHEEP SORREL (*Rumex acetosella* L.). U'uyuma (C). The leaves were pulverized, moistened with water, and eaten with salt. They were described as sour like vinegar.

GREEN DOCK (*Rumex conglomeratus* Murr.). Sapazü (C). The leaves were cooked and eaten as greens, but the seeds were not used.

TREE CLOVER (*Trifolium ciliatum* Nutt.). Olisa (C). This clover was eaten either raw or steamed. The steamed olisa was preserved as patciko (steamed clover dried for later use).

CLOVER (*Trifolium ciliolatum* Benth.). Patcuku (C), pa'tcūkū (S). This clover was steamed and thereafter eaten, or dried and stored.

COW CLOVER (*Trifolium involucratum* Ort.). Saksamö (C). A white-blossomed clover with vinegar flavor; eaten raw; never cooked or dried. Both leaves and flowers were eaten. If wilted or dry the leaves were soaked and stirred in a basket of cold water for ten minutes, making a sour drink.

TOMCAT CLOVER (*Trifolium tridentatum* Lindl.). Wilamü (C). Eaten, raw or steamed, before it bloomed. The leaves, stems, and buds were eaten. No pressing or blowing was required before eating the first of the season's crop. For storage the steamed leaves were spread out on *Wyethia helenioides* leaves, to dry in the sun for winter use. In winter the stored clover was either soaked in water or boiled before eating.

CLOVER (*Trifolium sp.*). Pumusayu (C). Eaten raw or steamed. Steamed clover dried for later use.

MULE-EARS (*Wyethia helenioides* Nutt.). Notopayu (C). Young shoots were eaten raw after peeling off the outer coating. They had a sweetish taste.

The following greens have not been identified: istawü (C), boiled; limisü (C), līmī′su (S), smells like cabbage when cooking; pa′kane (S); palatakina (C), a cotyledon, leaves eaten raw for sour taste and to offset thirst; patsü (C), a sweet clover eaten raw, blossom white with red base; pōma′nī (S); sikku (C), yellow-flowered clover, steamed, dried; tcī′ptca (S); to′lomu (S), a clover; tu′ltulu (N), dried for winter, when eaten moistened and salted to taste; witimo (C), collected in March; wo′utcka (S), a "wild cabbage," boiled.

MANZANITA

Manzanita berries of four species were crushed for sweet, unfermented cider (sakū′ta, P, N; sakē′ma, C, S; īsū′ta, S). The species are *Arbutus menziesii* (moko′lkine, C), the best and sweetest, *Arctostaphylos viscida, A. tomentosa* (e′ye, C), and *A. manzanita* (mo′kosū, C), the poorest. *A. patula* (palapala, C) was not used, it being eaten by bears, not people.

The manzanita berries were picked by hand directly into a burden basket, or into a flat sifting basket held under different parts of a bush while these were shaken. The twigs and leaves of *Eriogonum nudum* were used as a brush to clear the ground under manzanita bushes before knocking off the berries. They were used later also to brush the berries together.

The berries were either used at once for cider making or dried and stored for winter consumption. Before use they were winnowed to remove leaves and dirt. Sometimes winnowing was by tossing a handful in the air and blowing the waste from it.

In making cider the berries, sometimes after a brief boiling, were reduced to a coarse meal by grinding. The meal was placed in a winnowing basket set over a water-tight cooking basket. Water was then poured over it, a little at a time, percolating through until all the flavor was gone from the meal. This was ascertained by tasting. Finer particles of the meal passed into the lower basket, so the liquid was decanted. It was then ready to drink. It would keep without souring from two to four days. It was used as a refreshing drink, particularly in summer and at social gatherings.

Manzanita cider was sometimes employed as an appetizer. In such a case it was "dipped" with a plume stick (sō'ma, S). This was a short stick with several small hawk tail feathers lashed to one end. It was dipped in the cider and the beverage sucked from the feathers. This process was said to create appetite and cure stomach trouble. However, it was thought that the medicinal value lay in the hawk feathers.

Stems of Kentucky bluegrass (*Poa pratensis*), tepute (C), were also used as a brush to dip in manzanita cider, which was then sucked from the stems. The term soma (C) also applied to this device. It was applied also to a species of sedge *(Carex)* the stems of which were similarly used. Whether soma was originally a plant name or the name for this device is not clear.

Berries were chewed for the sake of the flavor, but not swallowed. The leaves were chewed to relieve stomachache and cramps.

BERRIES AND FRUITS

Relatively slight reliance was put upon berries and fruits as food supply, the Miwok, like other central Californians, putting the principal stress on seeds, greens, and bulbs. Of the eleven species recorded in addition to manzanita, eight were eaten raw, to-wit: nine-bark, *Physocarpus capitatus* (Pursh) Ktze. (hemekine, C); choke-cherries, *Prunus demissa*[26] (Nutt.) Dietr. (pisakene, C; pīha'kene, S), singers ate because "good for the voice;" wild plum, *Prunus subcordata*[26] Benth. (yotoña, C); wild Sierra currant, *Ribes nevadense* Kell. (hemekine, C); gooseberry, *Ribes roezlii* Regel. (kilili, C), winnowed, then pulverized in mortar to eliminate stickers; blackberry, *Rubus vitifolius*[27] C. & S. (lututuya, C); *Solanum xantii* Gray (watana, C); grape, *Vitis californica*[28] Benth. (tolmesu, C, the vine; kimisu, C, the grape), mashed with hands in basket.

[26]Chesnut, 356.
[27]Chesnut, 355.
[28]Chesnut, 369.

The three berries or fruits which were cooked were from the California laurel, the blue elderberry, and the toyon:

CALIFORNIA LAUREL (*Umbellularia californica* Nutt.[29]). Loko (C). The fruit was roasted in ashes and eaten.

BLUE ELDERBERRY (*Sambucus glauca* Nutt.[30]). Añta'iyu (C), a'ñtai (S). Elderberries were used as food, always cooked. A certain quantity was eaten in season, but a larger stock was dried for winter consumption. In winter they were occasionally recooked, though sometimes eaten without.

TOYON (*Photinia arbutifolia* Lindl.[31]). Koso (C). The large red clusters of edible berries underwent protracted preparation as food. A preliminary boiling was followed by baking in a deep narrow earth oven. To maintain the heat in the pit, a fire was kept two or three days around it, but not over it. Another method of preparation was to gather the ripe berries and store them in a basket for two months until they had softened. They were then parched with coals in a basket and eaten. Large coals were used so that the separation of the berries from the coals would be easy. The berries were eaten with seed meal. They are slightly puckery.

Of the seven species also utilized by the Pomo and Yuki, *Prunus demissa, Prunus subcordata, Rubus vitifolius, Vitis californica,* and *Sambucus glauca* were eaten raw, while *Umbellularia californica* and *Photinia arbutifolia* were cooked first.

NECTAR

Nectar (tcuya, C) of flowers was sipped sporadically and as a pastime, as among ourselves. The plants mentioned by informants were two species of "paint brush," *Castilleia parviflora* Bong. var. *douglasii* Jepson, and *Castilleia pinetorum* Fer., both called litcitci (C) or hummingbird. Two explanations of this name were given: (1) The plants were frequented by hummingbirds. (2) Part of the flower looked like a hummingbird's bill. To sip the nectar the flower was pulled apart.

FUNGI

A specimen of only one fungus was obtained for identification, the Sierra puffball *(Lycoperdon sculptum)*, called by the Central Miwok

---

[29]Chesnut, 349.
[30]Chesnut, 388.
[31]Chesnut, 355.

potokele and patapsi. This puffball was eaten cooked. Usually it was dried in the sun two or three days, pulverized in a mortar, stone-boiled, and eaten with acorn soup. The Yuki do not eat the edible *Lycoperdon* of their region.[32]

The other puffballs mentioned by informants were the awakayu (C), which is white inside, and the wunesati (C), which is yellow inside. They were eaten either raw or cooked.

A red-edged yellow tree fungus (elmayu, C), that grows shelf-like on the trunks of black oaks and water oaks, was eaten only after boiling, squeezing, and salting. If eaten raw it was poisonous and caused vomiting, but not death. A decoction of this fungus was drunk as a cathartic and a cure for rheumatism. The fungus was also used as a poultice. Presumably this fungus is of the genus *Polyporus,* which is highly esteemed by the Pomo.[33]

The other fungi mentioned by informants were mushrooms, of which only one is poisonous:

WHITE MUSHROOM. Helli (C). This species was described as a large white mushroom with straight cylindrical stem. It was boiled, either fresh or dried, and eaten with acorn soup. Mushrooms for drying and storage were shredded. Later when boiled for food they were salted. Sometimes dried mushrooms were pulverized and made into soup. Pressing and blowing of prospective eaters preceded the first eating of the new crop.

GIANT MUSHROOM. Atita (C). This is a huge mushroom, one foot in diameter and with bulging stem. Below, it is pale brown. It is prepared like the preceding.

Elapete (C). This mushroom is shaped like the atita, but is smaller. It is not poisonous, but to the Miwok had an unpleasant flavor. Italians, however, are said to eat it.

Kippisü (C). This is a small mushroom, reputed to taste like an onion. It is eaten both raw and cooked.

Sunokulu (C). This small mushroom grows in clusters. It is boiled before eating.

POISONOUS MUSHROOM. Seke (C). This mushroom looks like the atita except that it lacks the bulging stem. Death was the result of eat-

---

[32]Chesnut, 300.
[33]Chesnut, 300.

ing it, though an antidote was sometimes successful if only a very small quantity had been eaten.   The symptoms of poisoning were bleeding from the nose and mouth, and vomiting.   The antidote was a decoction made by boiling dried deer brains, which were usually on hand, as they had been preserved for preparing buckskin by roasting in hot ashes and pressing into cakes.   The drinking of the greasy fluid was said to stop the vomiting and bleeding.   If one ate seke in the woods there was little hope for him, though the quantity eaten made some difference. If a person ate but one mouthful a mile from home, he might reach home, but would be very sick before he arrived.

MEDICINES

When ill, the Miwok depended greatly on ceremonial and shamanistic curative practices.   Scarification and prolonged suction were the staple methods.   There were regular "doctors" who sang and sucked.   Set ceremonies were sometimes performed over the sick.   These acts were believed to have great curative value, combating the evil causes of sickness.   With these were used many herb medicines, called hūkī′ku (C). The ailments thus treated were numerous, and for some, informants mentioned several cures.   Certain of the remedies have modern features, such as the use of brandy, and certain plants used were introduced by Caucasians.   Stomachic affections and severe travail were treated with a plaster of hot ashes and moist earth.[34]

Sixty-seven plants medicinally used by the Miwok were identified. Six of these were also used medicinally by the Pomo and Yuki: *Achillaea millefolium* L.,[35] *Artemisia vulgaris* L. var. *heterophylla*[36] Jepson, *Eriodictyon californicum*[37] (H. & A.) Greene, *Quercus lobata*[38] Nee′, *Sambucus glauca*[39] Nutt., *Umbellularia californica*[40] Nutt.   Six species used medicinally by the Miwok were not so used by the Wailaki, Yuki, and (or) Pomo; *Datisca glomerata*[41] Brew. & Wats., used by the Miwok as a medicine, was employed by the Pomo as a fish poison. *Daucus pusillus*[42] Michx., used by the Miwok for snake bite, was em-

[34]Powers, 354.
[35]Chesnut, 391.
[36]Chesnut, 392.
[37]Chesnut, 381.
[38]Chesnut, 343.
[39]Chesnut, 388.
[40]Chesnut, 349.
[41]Chesnut, 370.
[42]Chesnut, 372.

ployed by the Wailaki as a gambling talisman and by them its use for snake bite was attributed to the Spaniards. The use of *Gymnogramma triangularis* Kaulf. as a medicine was also attributed by the Pomo at Ukiah to the Spaniards.[43] *Rosa californica*[44] C. & S. was not used as a medicine by the Yuki and only rarely as food. *Sanicula menziesii*[45] H. & A. was not used medicinally by the Wailaki, nor was *Solanum nigrum*[46] L.

The comparison of the Miwok list of medicinal plants with the Pomo, Yuki, and Wailaki list published by Chesnut seems to point to virtually independent development of the two pharmacopoeias, especially in view of the fact that less than ten per cent. of the Miwok plants are used by the above groups. No doubt this condition is in part attributable to certain of the Miwok species not occurring in Mendocino county, the habitat of these groups, and vice versa.

Accounts of the sixty-seven identified and fifteen unidentified plants, used medicinally by the Miwok, follow:

LOWLAND FIR (*Abies grandis* Lindl.). In case of colds and rheumatism, this is applied externally and internally, according to Powers.[47] This is presumably an introduced species, as it is native only to the coast region from Sonoma county northward.[48]

YARROW (*Achillaea millefolium* L. var.). Kamya (C), kama'iya (S), sepesepa (C). The leaves and flowers of this introduced plant were steeped and the resulting infusion drunk or applied externally. It was drunk for bad colds and, during the influenza epidemic of 1918-1919, was externally used. The mashed leaves, either green or dry, bound to a wound, are said to stop pain.

GIANT HYSSOP (*Agastache urticifolia* [Benth.] Ktze.). Lokotokoyi (C). Boiled and drunk for measles. Siti'la (C). A decoction of the leaves was drunk as a cure for rheumatism.

ANGELICA (*Angelica breweri* Gray.) The root was chewed as a headache cure and as a remedy for colds. To ward off snakes angelica was chewed and rubbed on the body, and a decoction of it drunk.

43Chesnut, 303.
44Chesnut, 354.
45Chesnut, 373.
46Chesnut, 387.
47Powers, 354.
48Jepson, 1910, 120.

DUTCHMAN'S PIPE (*Aristolochia californica* Torr.) Okise (C). This plant was steeped and the decoction drunk to cure colds.

WORMWOOD (*Artemisia vulgaris* L. var.). Kītci'ñu (N), kitciño (C). A decoction of the leaves of this plant was drunk to cure rheumatism. The leaves were worn in the nostrils by mourners when crying, the pungent odor clearing the head. The leaves were inserted in one nostril to cure headache and rubbed on the body to keep ghosts (sulesko, C) away. Small balls containing wormwood and other "medicine" plants was attached at intervals on a string and worn as a necklace to prevent dreaming of the dead. Also with such a necklace one might venture forth at night without fear of ghosts. For a month following a death, this wormwood necklace[49] (poko, C) was worn by the close relatives of the decedent, who also abstained from salt and meat. Wormwood was called the special plant of malevolent shamans or "poisoners" (tuyuku), because such were reputed to carry poison in wormwood leaves to avoid personal injury. Corpse handlers rubbed themselves with wormwood, otherwise they would be haunted by the ghost of the deceased.

MUGWORT (*Artemisia vulgaris* L. var. *heterophylla* Jepson). Used like *A. vulgaris*.

PURPLE MILKWEED (*Asclepias cordifolia* [Benth.] Jepson). The root was used as a medicine.

MILKWEED (*Asclepias speciosa* Torr.). Sū'kennu (C). A decoction of the root was taken in small doses to cure venereal diseases and was said to effect a cure quickly. For two days the discharge was greatly increased; then it gradually decreased until in four or five days a cure was effected. The milk was also applied to warts.

BALSAM ROOT (*Balsamorrhiza sagittata* Nutt.). Ho'tcōtca (C). The root of this plant was ground, boiled, cooled, and drunk for rheumatism, headache, or other pain. For rheumatism a small cupful was drunk and the patient covered, because of the profuse perspiration which followed.

CALIFORNIA BARBERRY (*Berberis pinnata* Lag.). Holo'metu (C). A decoction made from the root was drunk for heartburn, ague, con-

---

[49] One of these "mourning strings" is shown in plate LXIII, figure 2, though the contents of the balls was not ascertained from the wearer, a widow who was wearing it as a sign of mourning for her late husband who had died nearly a year previously. See section dealing with "mourning necklace."

sumption, and rheumatism; and the leaves were chewed as a preventive of ague, etc.

For cuts, wounds, and abrasions a small piece of the root was chewed and the resultant liquid placed in the injury. If put well down into a wound it prevented swelling. Cuts and bruises were washed with a decoction of the root. Each warrior carried a piece of this root. While travelling the root was chewed to ward off ague and other diseases.

CANCHALAGUA (*Centaurium exaltatum* [Griseb.] Wight). A decoction of the stems and leaves of this plant was drunk for toothache, stomachache, other internal pains, and consumption.

CANCHALAGUA (*Centaurium venustum* [Gray] Rob.). A decoction, made with brandy, of the flowers and leaves was drunk in modern times for pneumonia. A decoction made with water was drunk to abate fever and ague.

MOUNTAIN MISERY (*Chamaebatia foliolosa* Benth.). Kɪᴛkiti'su (N, C). Its leaves were steeped in hot water and the resulting tea drunk hot. It was used for rheumatism and for diseases manifested by skin eruptions. These are denoted by the generic term molazü and include chicken pox, measles, and smallpox. Such diseases were never treated by a shaman. The leaves of this plant were also used as an ingredient in medicines for the treatment of venereal diseases. For coughs and colds a decoction, sometimes with other herbs mixed, was drunk.

MEXICAN TEA (*Chenopodium ambrosioides* L.). Tistisu (C). This plant, either boiled or raw, was applied as a poultice to reduce swelling. It was also used in the mouth for toothache or an ulcerated tooth. For gonorrhea it was used as a wash and was injected into the affected parts. It was also used as a wash for rheumatic parts.

PIPE-STEM (*Clematis lasiantha* Nutt.). Wakilwakilu (C). Pulverized charcoal made from this plant was dusted on running sores and burns.

CYPRESS (*Cupressus sp.*). A decoction of the stems was drunk as a remedy for colds and rheumatism.

DURANGO ROOT (*Datisca glomerata* Brew. & Wats.). Isiñotayi (C). The root was pulverized and a decoction made. This was used as a wash for sores and rheumatism.

TOLGUACHA (*Datura meteloides* DC). Monayu (C), mō'nūya (S). Shamans sometimes ate the root or drank a decoction of this plant to induce a delirium, during which they ran about wildly and saw strange visions. It was supposed to give them supernatural power and the ability to look into the future. Although in general use among the Yokuts, the adjacent Miwok seem never to have adopted its use, except as mentioned above.

RATTLESNAKE WEED (*Daucus pusillus* Michx.). Yotcitayu (C). This plant was chewed and placed on a snake bite. Perhaps this use was after Spanish example.[50]

SCOURING-RUSH (*Equisetum sp.*). The stems were used for medicine.

FLEABANE (*Erigeron foliosus* Nutt. var. *stenophyllus* Gray). We'ne (C). A boiled and cooled decoction of the washed and pounded root was drunk to abate fever and ague. In case of toothache a bit of the root was chewed and placed in the cavity. Fleabane came from the north ("Klamath River") by trade, and was paid for in beads, shells, and baskets.

YERBA SANTA, MOUNTAIN BALM (*Eriodictyon californicum* [H. & A.] Greene). Pa'ssalu (C). The leaves and flowers were steeped in hot water and the resulting tea drunk to abate coughs, colds, stomach ache, and rheumatism. Sometimes the leaves were chewed for the same purpose. Also they were warmed and used as plasters on aching or sore spots, the natural stickiness of the leaves making them adhere readily. In the form of a cigarette the leaves were smoked to relieve coughs and colds. Mashed leaves of the mountain balm were applied to cuts, wounds, and abrasions; and also over fractured bones, in order to keep down the swelling, aid the knitting, and relieve pain.

GOLDEN YARROW (*Eriophyllum caespitosum* Dougl.). Lakma, pusukele (C). The leaves were bound on the body over aching parts.

RATTLESNAKE WEED (*Euphorbia ocellata* D. & H.). Pē'sippēsa (N), pē'sippesa (C). The leaves were mashed and rubbed into a snake bite. It was stated that the milky juice struck in and prevented swelling. A decoction was drunk as a blood purifier.

---

[50]Chesnut, 372.

THYME-LEAF SPURGE (*Euphorbia serpyllifolia* Pers.). Running sores were washed with a decoction of the leaves of this plant, after which a green powder made from the leaves of *Solidago californica* Nutt. was dusted on the sores. *Euphorbia serpyllifolia* was said to cure rattlesnake bites if applied immediately.

SWEET-SCENTED BEDSTRAW (*Galium triflorum* Michx.). Tutumkalali (C). This was boiled and drunk as a tea, for dropsy.

INCISED CRANESBILL (*Geranium incisum* Nutt.). Olosena (C). The root was pulverized and steeped. The decoction was rubbed on aching joints, but not on open sores.

CALIFORNIA EVERLASTING (*Gnaphalium decurrens* Ives var. *californicum* Gray). Hū'semelaiyu. The pungent leaves of this plant were bound on any swelling as a poultice. Yutañyutañü (C). The flowers and leaves were used as a poultice, after heating in a fire to make them sticky. Potokpota (C). A decoction of the leaves was drunk for colds and stomach trouble.

GUM PLANT (*Grindelia robusta* Nutt.). Kalkala (C). The leaves were steeped and the decoction used to wash running sores. The steeped material was also pulverized and applied to sores.

GOLD FERN (*Gymnogramma triangularis* Kaulf.). Pilpilka (C). This was chewed for toothache, care being taken to keep the quid near the troublesome tooth.

TREE HAPLOPAPPUS (*Haplopappus arborescens* Hall). Tce'ktceka, susube (C). The boiled decoction of the leaves was drunk hot to cure stomach trouble and applied to rheumatic parts. During menstruation and after parturition women sometimes drank it to relieve pain. It was too strong a remedy to be used during parturition.

The twigs and leaves were bound on rheumatic parts without mashing. The leaves were applied to boils to bring them to a head. They might also be bound over a sore on one's foot when travelling, being tied with a piece of buckskin or put inside the moccasin.

HEDGE-LEAVED HAPLOPAPPUS (*Haplopappus cuneatus* Gray). A decoction of the stems was drunk for colds.

TARWEED (*Hemizonia virgata* Gray). Kitimpa, tū'mō (C). A bath with a decoction of this plant was used for measles and for fevers in general. It must never be taken internally. From another species of tarweed a decoction was made which was drunk as a headache cure.

GOLD-WIRE (*Hypericum concinnum* Benth.). Hoyilü (C). Boiled and used as wash for running sores.

CHEESE-WEED (*Malva parviflora* L.). Kasani (C). The leaves, soft stems, and flowers were steeped and used as a poultice on running sores, boils, and swellings.

SPEARMINT (*Mentha spicata* L.). Sisimela (C). A hot tea of the boiled leaves was drunk to relieve stomach trouble and diarrhoea, and apparently also purely as a beverage.

BUENA MUJER (*Mentzelia sp.*) Matcū' (C). The pulverized seeds were mixed with water, or preferably fox or wild cat grease, and applied as a poultice.

MONKEY FLOWER (*Mimulus sp.*). The root of a shrubby yellow *Mimulus* was used to make a tea with astringent properties, used as a cure for diarrhoea.

MUSTANG MINT (*Monardella lanceolata* Gray). A decoction of the leaves, upper stems, and flowers was drunk for colds and for headache.

MOUNTAIN PENNYROYAL (*Monardella odoratissima* Benth.). Hukume (C). A decoction of the stems and flower heads was drunk for colds and fevers and was also imbibed at times as a beverage.

WHITE NAVARRETIA (*Navarretia cotulaefolia* [Benth.] H. & A.). Potela (C). Boiled, and decoction applied to swelling.

SNAKE ROOT (*Osmorrhiza sp.*). Kawibe (C). Chewed and put on snake bite.

BIRD'S-FOOT FERN (*Pellaea ornithopus* Hook.). Pē'sippēsa (N). Steeped in hot water and tea drunk to stop nose-bleed. Also drunk as a spring medicine and blood purifier.

SMALL-FLOWERED BEARD-TONGUE (*Pentstemon breviflorus* (Lindl.). Lulusu (C). Steeped and drunk for colds.

VARIOUS-LEAVED BLUEBELL (*Phacelia heterophylla* Pursh).

Tawimuyu (C). This plant, dried, was pulverized and put in fresh wounds.

HORNED MILKWORT (*Polygala cornuta* Kell.). Kitma (C). A strong, very bitter decoction of this plant served as an emetic. In dilute form it was used for coughs, colds, and pains.

KNOTWEED, ALPINE SMARTWEED (*Polygonum bistortoides* Pursh). Kaima (C). The root was mashed and used as a poultice on sores and boils.

MOUNTAIN MINT (*Pycnanthemum californicum* Torr.). Holoyu (C). This was boiled as a tea for colds.

WHITE OAK (*Quercus lobata* Neé). The outer bark (masakuta, C), pulverized in a bedrock mortar, was dusted on running sores after thorough cleansing; used particularly for sore umbilicus in babies. A bitter decoction of the bark was drunk as a cough medicine.

INTERIOR LIVE OAK (*Quercus wislizenii* A.DC.). Pulverized bark used like that of the *Q. lobata*.

CASCARA[51] (*Rhamnus rubra* Greene). Lo'o (N). A decoction of the bark was drunk as a cathartic.

WILD ROSE (*Rosa californica* C. & S.). Mamute (C). The leaves and berries were steeped and drunk as medicine for pains, colic, etc.

GREEN DOCK (*Rumex conglomeratus* Murr.). Sapazü (C). The root was pulverized and boiled. The decoction was drunk and the boiled root applied externally, for the cure of boils.

BLUE ELDERBERRY (*Sambucus glauca* Nutt.). For ague a decoction made from the blossoms was drunk, taken as soon as possible after the shaking began. The patient was covered, as profuse perspiration followed.

POISON SANICLE (*Sanicula bipinnata* H. & A.). Wene (C). This plant was boiled and applied to snake bite.

PURPLE SANICLE (*Sanicula bipinnatifida* Dougl.). Wene (C). A

---

[51]It was the use of this bark by the California tribes which first brought this remedy to the attention of physicians with the result that it has been regularly adopted as *a remedy* and is now in quite general use.

cure all. Root boiled and decoction drunk. The steeped leaves were also applied to snake bite.

GAMBLE WEED (*Sanicula menziesii* H. & A.). Lawati huzikus (C). Literally (?) "rattlesnake medicine." The pulverized leaves were placed on rattlesnake bites and other wounds. It was never drunk as a tea, as it caused sickness.

SKULLCAP (*Scutellaria angustifolia* Pursh). A decoction was used as a wash for sore eyes.

SKULLCAP (*Scutellaria sp.*). Wenene (C). Boiled, and decoction drunk for coughs and colds.

WILD RYE (*Sitanion sp.*). Pokute (C). Used dry or green by shaman to strike patient with, before and after sucking.

BLACK NIGHTSHADE (*Solanum nigrum* L.). Ma'nmantca (S). A decoction was used as a wash for sore eyes.

COMMON GOLDENROD (*Solidago californica* Nutt.). Lo'yama (S). A small quantity of a decoction was held in the mouth to alleviate toothache. It was expectorated, never swallowed. A pale green powder was made from the leaves and applied to open sores after washing with a decoction of *Euphorbia serpyllifolia*.

PITCHER SAGE (*Sphacele calycina* Benth.). Watakka'iyu (C). A decoction of the leaves of this plant was drunk to abate fever, ague, and headache. One cupful was the dose and it was often sufficient to cure. One informant gave the following example: Before the whites came to Tuolumne county an old Indian brought watermelon seeds from Mission San Jose. He planted these near the Tuolumne (?) river, about eight miles west of French Bar. Soon after the Indians ate the melons they had ague, and cured themselves with pitcher sage.

SNOWBERRY (*Symphoricarpos albus* [L.] Blake). Yutasena (C). The root was pounded and steeped to make a decoction, which was drunk to alleviate colds and stomachache.

VINEGAR WEED, CAMPHOR WEED (*Trichostema lanceolatum* Benth.). Tcūkū'tcū (C). A decoction of the leaves and flowers was drunk for colds, malaria, headache, ague, general debility, and stricture of the bladder. A bath with this decoction was a preventive measure against ague and smallpox. If the bath was nct employed in time to prevent smallpox, then the patient was bathed with a decoction made from the large, flat leaves of the incense cedar. This cured the pustules and prevented serious eruptions of the skin. With this should be drunk a decoction of the root of *Erigeron foliosus stenophyllus*. Many people were said to have been saved by this treatment in the epidemic of 1875. Sitting over a steaming decoction of vinegar weed was a cure for uterine trouble. It should not be used during pregnancy. The leaves of vinegar weed were chewed and placed in the cavity of or around an aching tooth.

CALIFORNIA LAUREL (*Umbellularia californica* Nutt.). Loko (C). The leaves and twigs were bound on the forehead as a cure for headache.

NETTLE (*Urtica gracilis* Ait. var.). Two rheumatism remedies were obtained from this nettle. A decoction was made of the root and with it the rheumatic part was bathed. The powdered leaves were sometimes rubbed on the affected part and produced a fiery itching. The decoction was the preferred remedy.

NETTLE (*Urtica gracilis* Ait. var. *holosericea* Jepson). Sosolo'yū. To relieve certain pains the affected part was struck with a branch of nettle.

MULE EARS (*Wyethia angustifolia* Nutt.). Hū'ssūpu (N), hotcotca (C). A decoction of the leaves was used as a bath for fever patients and produced a profuse perspiration, so that the patient must be covered immediately. It was never taken internally because poisonous.

MEXICAN BALSAMEA (*Zauschneria californica* Presl.). Husī'ku (C). In cases of tuberculosis ("vomit blood") a decoction of the leaves was drunk; also drunk as a cathartic, and for kidney and bladder trouble. It was used by women after parturition, probably to stop hemorrhages. It was also used for "syphilis"; and one informant described a case in which his treatment of a severely afflicted Mexican resulted in such relief in four days that the patient was able to walk with ease.

The following plants used as remedies have not been identified:

Hokisa (C). A plant imported from the north where it was also smoked to keep the ghost away at a funeral. It was also drunk as a tea. Its root was rubbed on dancers, except those who danced aletu, helkiku, and helkiböksu. The root was also rubbed on the body as a rheumatism cure, to prevent snake bites, and to prevent seeing "devils."

Hū'kūme (C). For coughs and colds a decoction of the leaves and flowers of this plant was drunk.

Husīku hekapūsuna (C). Literally "medicine wash." This is a small plant with milky juice. Any sore was washed with a tea made from it, and then sprinkled with powdered leaves of *Solidago californica*. One informant said it would cure rattlesnake bite if applied immediately. The plant grows in the middle or late summer in a small rosette in dry rocky soil in the foothills. It is said to be killed by rain.

Hū'ssūpu (N, C). A bath in a decoction of the leaves of this plant was a fever remedy which produced a profuse perspiration, so that the patient had to be immediately covered. It was never taken internally, because poisonous. The plant grows about two feet high and has red flowers.

Metmeti (C). A plant obtained by trade and used as medicine.

Pa'kkīlu (C). The charcoal from this tree was dusted on running sores and burns.

Sepesepa (C). This plant was made into a tea which was drunk for stomach trouble and also used as an eye wash.

Sokloikine (C). A bulbous plant like an onion, which was rubbed on the body and eaten, to keep rattlesnakes away.

тama' (N, C). The leaves of this plant were pulled from the stems and soaked in cold water. The resultant sour liquid was drunk as a fever remedy. The seeds were pounded, mixed with water, and drunk for an appetizer.

Tasina (C). A plant used to lay on a rattlesnake bite after it had been scratched with obsidian. The doctor sang a little and the patient usually got well.

Wild cucumber. Ta'wûkna (S). A decoction of this plant was drunk to cure venereal diseases.

тe'peltēpelu (C). The root of this umbelliferous plant was mashed, boiled, and drunk warm for internal venereal complications, presumably in the bladder. When cool the decoction might be used as a pain killer to bathe any part which was painful. It was used for rheumatism.

Tu'ltulu (N). For stomach trouble and as a "pain killer" a decoction of the root was drunk.

Wakā'lī (C). The dried root was pulverized and boiled with a little water. The moist, cooled material was then bound on a swelling, which it reduced rapidly. It was never placed on cuts or abrasions, or taken internally, because poisonous.

Wakáliñu hūsī'ku (C). The Miwok name means literally "rattlesnake medicine." The pulverized seeds were bound or dusted on a snake bite to prevent swelling.

PLANTS NOT USED

Of interest equal to the utilized plants are sixty named but not utilized, of which forty-seven have been completely identified. Whether all are actually inedible is not known, nor is it known if some time in the past the Miwok have experimented with these and discovered that they could not be utilized as food. Of the forty-seven plants, however, seven are utilized by the Yuki and Pomo,[52] to-wit: *Alnus rhombifolia*[53] Nutt. for dye, medicine, arrows, and tinder; *Amelanchier alnifolia*[54] Nutt. for food and arrows; *Helenium puberulum*[55] DC. for medicine; *Lonicera interrupta*[56] Benth. for nectar, medicine, and basketry; *Rhamnus californica*[57] Esch., *Rhus diversiloba*[58] T. & G. for food (leaves), medicine, wrapping for food in earth oven, basketry, and skin paint; *Lithophragma affinis*[59] Gray for medicine.

Two unused Miwok plants, *Sonchus asper* L. and *Lotus strigosus* (Nutt.) Greene, were used by the Luiseño as greens.[60]

The plants recorded as not used by the Miwok are the following:

Alnus rhombifolia Nutt. (pamalu, C); *Amelanchier alnifolia* Nutt. (yossina, C); *Antennaria argentea* Benth. (potokpota. C); *Arctostaphylos patula* Greene (palapala, C); *Barbarea vulgaris* (L) R. Br. (soso-

[52]Chesnut, Plants used by the Indians of Mendocino County, California, 295-408.
[53]Chesnut, 332.
[54]Chesnut, 355.
[55]Chesnut, 394.
[56]Chesnut, 388.
[57]Chesnut, 368.
[58]Chesnut, 364.
[59]Chesnut, 353.
[60]Sparkman, 228, 231.

wina, C) ; *Brassica sp.* (wimeya, C) ; *Brodiaea volubilis* (Kell.) Baker (wakilwakilu, C) ; *Bromus rubens* L. (tcuppayu, C), stickers a nuisance to people wearing moccasins; *Calyptridium umbellatum* (Torr.) Greene (paipaiyu, C) ; *Carduus sp.* (yotcta, C) ; *Ceanothus cordulatus* Kell. (cenebe, C), eaten by deer; *Collinsia tinctoria* Hartw. (tcata lawati, C, literally "rattlesnake's rattle," and istamü, C) ; *Collinsia torreyi* Gray (osta, C) ; *Collomia grandiflora* Dougl. (witcima, C) ; *Cryptanthe affinis* Greene (sosolina, C) ; *Cryptanthe sp.* (susu) ; *Epilobium adenocaulon* Haussk. (tcêpise) ; *Epilobium sp.* (samlili) ; *Fontinalis sp.* (tcepekula) ; *Funaria hygrometrica* (tcepekuda, C) ; *Gilia achillaefolia* Mason (lelema, C) ; *Gilia androsacea* Steud. var. *montana* (suppatawa, C) ; *Habenaria unalaschensis* (Spreng.) Wats. (sasi, C), a poisonous plant which caused blood vomiting if eaten; *Helenium bigelovii* Gray (hangu, C) ; *Helenium puberulum* DC. (polobia, C) ; *Juncus sp.* (kokoyu, C) ; *Kelloggia galioides* Torr. (pusukulu, C) ; *Lithophragma affinis* Gray (epesenu, C) ; *Lonicera interrupta* Benth. (wa'kilwakīlu, C) ; *Lotus oblongifolius* (Benth.) Greene (lulumati, C) ; *Lotus strigosus* (Nutt.) Greene (cikasi, C) ; *Lotus torreyi* Gray (susuyi, C) ; *Marrubium vulgare* L. (yotcitayu, C) ; *Mimulus sp.* (yasaññaña, C) ; *Œnothera strigosa* Willd. (sonta, C) ; *Osmaronia cerasiformis* (T. & G.) Greene (poloyina, C) ; *Peucedanum sp.* (sumsümi, C) ; *Pentstemon heterophyllus* Lindl. (yutumpula, C) ; *Plantago lanceolata* L. (supa, C) ; *Potentilla glandulosa* Lindl. (yatcatca, C), although not poisonous, informants said seeds not eaten because too few to gather; *Polygonum lapathifolium* L. (tcostowina, C) ; *Populus tremuloides* Michx. (taktakkalu, C) ; *Rhamnus californica* Esch. (lo'o, C) ; *Rhus diversiloba,* T.&G. (nukusu, C) ; *Rudbeckia sp.* (mika, C) ; *Salix sp.* (sisima, C) ; *Sarcodes sanguinea* Torr. (hokolpate, C), plucked because of beauty; *Scutellaria bolanderi* Gray (susupe, C) ; *Senecio triangularis* Hook. (yusuyi, C) ; *Sidalcea glaucescens* Greene (lotowiye, C) ; *Silene californica* Dur. (pusulu, C), rats eat seeds; *Sonchus asper* L. (tcitimpa, C) ; *Symphoricarpos rotundifolius* Gray (mokolkine, C) ; *Taraxacum officinale* Weber (natumnatumma, C) ; *Trifolium pratense* L. (yenwa, C) ; *Verbascum blattaria* L. (yotowina, C) ; *Viola adunca* Sm. (sitimpa, C).

Completely unidentified: sepekula, (C), a lichen; elapete and seke, mushrooms.

The attitude of mind toward the unused species of the plant world is perhaps well indicated by an aged informant. When asked if a species of *Polygonum* was harmful, she said she did not know and was afraid to try unknown things. Yet sometime in the past there must have been an initial trial of each species used.

TAKING OF MAMMALS

Formerly, Mule Deer *(Odocoileus hemionus)* were abundant in the hills and mountains of Miwok territory. Dwarf Elk *(Cervus nannodes)* were found in the foothills and in the delta. On the plains were Pronghorn Antelope *(Antilocapra americana)*. The Central Miwok, at least, formerly journeyed to the plains country, in Yokuts territory, to hunt the antelope.

Hunters sweated and bathed to eliminate the human odor before hunting deer. Perhaps, too, it had the magical significance of creating ceremonial purity. The body was rubbed with the root of *Angelica breweri* to give a "pleasing odor" and to counteract the human odor, which might be detected by the quarry. Also it was supposed to confer good luck on the hunter. If a hunter did not get deer, he steamed and bathed himself with a decoction of wild sunflower root *(Balsamorrhiza sagittata),* pulverized in a mortar. The boiling was done in a basket with a red-hot quartz stone, as big as one's fist. The man knelt beside the basket. Over him and the basket were placed the necessary deer hides to confine the steam. He held his head over the basket until the liquid cooled somewhat. Then he washed all over with the decoction. This treatment was taken in the dwelling house.

DEER. The deer, üwü'ya (P, N), *u*wü'ya (C, S), was the most important food mammal. It was taken in several ways. Special nets, about forty feet in length, were made for catching deer. One of these was stretched across each of the several runways in any given vicinity. One end was fastened securely to a tree, the opposite end being kept taut by means of a rope held by a man on watch, who was carefully concealed on the leeward side of the runway, so that the approaching animal could not get his scent. Men beat the bush and drove the deer toward the nets. As a deer ran into the almost invisible net the watcher slackened his rope enough for the animal to become thoroughly entangled, when he dispatched it with a club. Sometimes a snare was set between two posts on a deer trail, so that the first deer passing was ensared, either by the foot or the antlers.

The deer migrated by well-known trails from higher to lower altitudes in September and October, returning again in April and May. At these times they were caught by means of a long brush fence, usually V-shaped, built where the lay of the land permitted, with a small opening at some advantageous point, as at the angle of the V. Within easy arrow range a pit was dug and roofed over with brush and earth, to protect and conceal the hunter. Here a small fire of mountain live oak (saka'sa, C), was built and the coals covered to preserve the heat, especially during the night. It served as a deodorizer. It provided warmth for the hunter to heat his hands and keep them nimble and ready to shoot accurately. Just at the opening through the fence was placed a young oak bough with mistletoe (ti'ñtīla, C), of which the deer are very fond. This food arrested the attention of the animal long enough to allow a good heart shot.

A Southern Miwok form of deer trap consisted of a V-shaped brush fence with a small corral at the angle of the V. There were three or four small openings in the corral, in which strong snares were set, each attached to a tree or to a fairly heavy log. The rope was long enough for a captive deer to move about somewhat and, when a drag was used, the deer could run some distance. Near the entrance to the corral were small pits in which men were concealed, so that, as the deer neared the corral, the men cut off their retreat. The deer bolting for the openings in the corral, were ensnared, and easily dispatched with arrows or clubs.

Another method of taking deer was by driving them over a precipice. Still another method was for the hunter to conceal himself under boughs in a pit beside a deer trail. As the deer passed at night to their drinking place he shot them. Sometimes deer were driven by ten or twelve men toward an archer stationed on a little hill or rock near the deer trail.

Communal daylight hunts were undertaken by members of a single hamlet (nena, C). Small fires, built by several men, were set in the hills around a meadow, into which deer went. These men kept building new fires. The hunters were concealed behind trees and brush. As the deer descended to the meadow they approachd the fires from curiosity. Then the concealed hunters shot them with the bow and arrows. As there was no noise the deer took no alarm. They were also shot from ambush, as they endeavored to escape along the trails from small fires set for the purpose of driving them out. Deer were particularly sought where the Deer Brush *(Ceanothus integerrimus)*, ūsū'nni (C, S), grew, and upon which they fed.

Several devices were employed in stalking deer. A tight-fitting cap (ko'llī, P. N) of grass disguised the hunter as he crawled toward his prey. A deer mask (sūki'ppū, P, N) was also used. It consisted of the entire skin of the deer, worn by the hunter so that the eyeholes permitted him to see easily. The hunter imitated the movements of a deer and approached against the wind. He followed closely the actions of the herd, even simulating fright when the herd was startled. Sometimes he even attracted the jealous attention of a buck. He was thus able to follow the herd and kill one deer after another with his noiseless arrows. To aid, a hunter often carried a small branch in front of him, as he crept stealthily upon the game. Often, to reduce the weight of the mask, the antlers were replaced by forked oak sticks, darkened by charring. Magic properties were believed to attach to this mask. It was used secretly and kept from supposed pollution by contact with women and children.

Sometimes a cluster of pine stems, suggesting antlers, was placed on the disguised hunter's head. Such clusters were found growing at squirrel nests in pine trees. The hunter used this disguise in the fall, when the bucks would approach to attack him and thus offer easy marks for his arrows. The hunter, on all fours, twisted his head sidewise like a buck to enrage the buck. If the animal came close enough, the hunter stabbed it with a pointed staff of mountain mahogany. Otherwise he shot it with an arrow. Mountain Lions *(Felis oregonensis)* did not bother the disguised deer hunter, but bears did. One hunter in disguise killed four bears in two days. Two were young, but the other two were old and tried to kill and eat him. Still another stalking disguise was a complete covering of the body with the vine of the "wild cucumber" called ta'wûkna (S). This was employed in stalking antelope also.

Deer were also run down. A large buck was followed all day. Then the hunter slept for the night. Starting at dawn the next day, he would be likely to overtake his quarry in the afternoon. A fast runner could tire a deer in a day. Dogs were not usually employed in this connection, because they made the deer wild. Sometimes very fat deer and wounded deer were run down by dogs.

There was no special treatment of dead deer. Dogs might eat deer meat without causing the hunter ill luck. The Miwok lacked the observances and restrictions that prevailed in these matters in northwestern California.

Deer were skinned on the ground, not suspended. A sharp-edged piece of tibia was used as a skinning tool. Usually deer were skinned after being brought home. The viscera, however, were removed where the animal was killed. The stomach was given to a companion of the hunter, especially an older man. It was cooked at once, being covered with damp earth, ashes, coals, and on top of all a slow fire. It was cooked for two hours. In it were placed the cleaned entrails, windpipe, lights, and longitudinal pieces of flesh from near the kidneys. Blood also was added. After cooking, the stomach was tied in a bundle with willow or chaparral twigs and fastened to a stick, so that it might be carried over the shoulder.

The liver was given to some old woman, such a one as had always given the hunter acorn mush when she made it. The liver was considered a delicacy. It was boiled in a basket. The hunter's mother-in-law and wife reserved the sirloin, which was cooked on the coals for them by the hunter, his mother, or his grandmother. It was not proper for his mother-in-law or wife to cook it. The cooking was done within the dwelling. If there were more people to eat the meat than there was room for, some were fed outdoors.

The forelegs and hind legs were given by the hunter to relatives and neighbors. The body was given to his wife's relatives (brother, father, etc.), also to son-in-law and daughter-in-law. The hunter ate but little himself. Being a good hunter, all brought him seed meal (tuyu) and he was plentifully supplied with that. Of course, a hunter had relatives by marriage and neighbors who reciprocated, so that he was usually amply supplied with venison. If a hunter kept what he killed he was looked down upon.

When all men of the hamlet hunted, the kill was divided among them, regardless of whether some got deer or not. Meanwhile the women prepared acorns and other vegetable foods, and regaled the hunters with all sorts of delicacies.

The earth oven was sometimes used for cooking deer meat.

ELK (haka'ia, P, N, C) and antelope (ha'lū, P; ha'lūsū, N; halus, C) were stalked with the deer mask. No special elk or antelope mask was made, and these animals were not snared as were deer. The Central Miwok hunted elk in the lower foothills, the mountaineers descending to hunt without interference. Elk were also hunted by the Plains Miwok in the delta region.

ANTELOPE. In hunting antelope ten or fifteen men went together. Some of the party deployed to right and left of the antelope, so as to bring them into range for the rest of the party. Often three or four antelope were cut out in this fashion.

BEAR. Both the American Black Bear *(Ursus americanus)* and the Grizzly Bear *(Ursus henshawi)* were eaten by the mountaineers, but not by the Plains Miwok. There appears to have been no special device for hunting the bear. A party of at least a dozen hunters systematically pursued a bear and killed him with their bows and arrows.

RABBITS. Next perhaps in importance to the deer as food animals were the rabbits. Both the Jackrabbit (epa′lī, P; eplálī, N, C, S), *Lepus californicus,* and the Cottontails (hī′ga, P; hīka′kû, N; тo′ssebe, C), *Sylvilagus auduboni, S. nuttallii, S. bachmani,* were caught, chiefly by means of the rabbit net, especially in the summer. The net was set either in a straight line or in V-shape, being held in place by forked greasewood sticks. Sometimes it was stretched around the base of a hill. It was three or four feet high and three hundred to four hundred yards in length. The rabbits were driven into this net, often by the whole populace of the village. Men were stationed at convenient intervals along the net, to club the rabbits as they became entangled. Among the Northern Miwok these men hid behind trees thirty or forty yards from the net, then ran forward to seize the entangled rabbits and break their necks.

In the higher mountains, where the snow was deep, rabbits were taken in the winter by pursuing them on snowshoes and killing them with clubs. In the mountain region also rabbits were decoyed by placing the fingers on the lips and imitating the cry of distress of a young rabbit. This brought the older rabbits within easy range of the bow and arrow.

BEAVER. The Golden Beaver (he′nnit, P. N), *Castor canadensis,* was taken by first burning off the tule around its pond. This exposed the entrances to the beaver houses and left a clear field in which to dig out the animal. It was usually dispatched with a club, but if it tried to escape, the cleared pond made it an easy mark for the bow and arrow.

SQUIRRELS. California Gray Squirrels *(Sciurus griseus)* were shot with the bow and arrow. A snare was of little avail, because they would gnaw it. California Ground Squirrels *(Citellus beecheyi)* were not eaten so much as gray squirrels. They, too, were shot with the bow. Also they were captured by dogs. Their flesh was not preserved.

RATS were killed by means of an acorn fixed under a stone, so that when gnawed the stone fell on the rat.

TAKING OF BIRDS

QUAIL. The most important food birds to the hill Miwok were the Valley Quail (nükü'te, P; heke'ke, N, C, S), *Lophortyx californica,* and the Mountain Quail (kū'yaka, P; kūyaya, ū'yakka, C; hū'yūkūī, hū'yūhūī, S), *Oreortyx picta.* They were taken chiefly by means of a brush fence with openings five to ten feet apart, in which were set snares (po'kī, P; we'lla, S). Such a fence was built in any desired shape, governed by its situation. It was ordinarily about three feet high and

Fig. 23.—Brush fence snare.

composed of vertical stakes driven into the ground, with twigs or brush interwoven. It was usually built near or around a spring. In the latter case a brush roof was placed over it. Further, any other convenient supply of water was covered with fine grass or pine needles. This drove many birds, including quail, to seek the openings in the fence.

The snare was made of human hair twisted into a very fine, but strong, thread. As shown in text-figure 23, each opening in the fence had a pair of crossed sticks to which the snare was attached, by very lightly tying it to the point at which the sticks crossed, or to one of them, or by looping it over slight notches cut on the two sticks. These were simply means for holding open the loop of the snare, the opposite end being firmly attached to any convenient branch or stake. The slight notches in the side sticks usually had to be renewed after a quail was caught, because of the damage done by its struggles. No attempt was made to hang and strangle the bird by means of a spring pole. It found itself caught by head, wing, or foot and worried itself to death in its endeavor to gain freedom. A quail fence was used year after year with whatever repairs were necessary. The vicinity of a small streamlet, called "Indian spring" (Kolakota), lying 200 or 300 yards up the canyon from the steatite quarry Lotowayaka, near the modern town of Tuolumne, was a favorite place for erecting a quail fence. The exact site of the fence was the crest of a steep ridge just northeast of the streamlet. As many as fifty quail a day were caught in spring when migrating to higher altitudes. Another fence on a hill northeast of Tuolumne was said to have been half a mile long.

Nets of human hair and, in Caucasian times, of horse hair were stretched across a hillside up which quail habitually walked. There were openings in the net which led into pockets, flanked by sticks to hold them in position. The quail tried to go through the openings and became entangled in the pockets of the net.

BAND-TAILED PIGEONS (luñuti, C), *Columba fasciata,* were caught in a fence built around a spring near scrub oaks. The pigeons after drinking, were accustomed to walk from the spring to the scrub oak patch for small acorns. They tried to pass through the openings in the fence and became ensnared. Twelve to fifty a day could be caught. Pigeons and other birds were shot with arrows from a green brush blind (ū'spu, P) built at a spring. Squabs were never used for decoys as among the Yokuts of Tule river.[61] Pigeons were usually eaten at once, not preserved.

PIGEONS, JAYS, RED-SHAFTED FLICKERS *(Colaptes cafer)*, and an unidentified red-breasted bird (TAKANA, S) were caught in a noose trap baited with an acorn placed between four vertical sticks (text-figure 24). A fifth stick, serving as a trigger, had the noose attached to it.

Fig. 24.—Baited snare.

The end of the trigger stick was placed on the acorn. When the bird pecked at the acorn the trigger was dislodged, the trap sprung, and the bird hung by the spring pole. A single hunter could set as many as two hundred snares in a day. He visited them frequently and might secure a basketful of birds during the day. It was necessary to remove all ensnared birds before night, as the coyotes would eat them and destroy the traps.

WOODPECKERS. An ingenious method of catching woodpeckers was

[61]Holmes, 1902, pl. 32.

recorded. During the day the people plugged all, except a few, of the woodpecker holes in the trees of a given grove or restricted locality. In the few remaining holes the woodpeckers congregated at nightfall and were an easy prey to the hunters who ascended the trees during the night.

WATERFOWL. To the Plains Miwok waterfowl were an important item of diet. Two kinds of duck traps were made. In one of these,

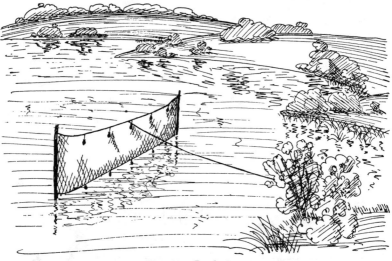

Fig. 25.—Duck trap.

two poles were set up in the shallow, still water near the shore of a lake or stream where the ducks were wont to feed. Between them was stretched a net (sammi, P, N) about six feet wide and forty or more feet long (text-figure 25). The edges were weighted slightly and to the middle of the upper edge was attached a long cord which ran to the hiding place of the watcher in the neighboring tule or tall grass. Acorns were used as bait, since these sink to the bottom. At first a duck or two might discover the bait and commence feeding. This attracted others and soon a large flock was swimming and diving for the bait. When a sufficient number were in the proper position, the watcher gave a careful, strong pull on the line. This caused the net to fall flat on the water. The first impulse of the ducks was to fly away rather than to dive. Immediately they tried to rise they became entangled in the meshes and the watcher easily caught them. The weights on both edges of the net held it down quite firmly.

The other duck trap was designed to catch the birds as they winged just above the water. It consisted of the same kind of a net as that just described, supported at one end by a post or a tree, the other end being attached to a rope which ran up and over a crotched post to a blind or some other point of concealment for the watcher. When set the rope was loose and the net lay relaxed near the surface of the water. Upon

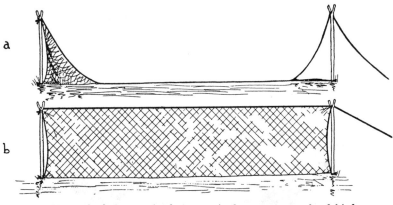

Fig. 26.—a, duck trap, set.   b, trap raised upon approach of birds.

the approach of a flock of ducks to within a short distance of the trap the watcher raised the net suddenly by a strong pull on the rope. The ducks flew into the almost invisible net before they could change their course. As they struck the net the line was relaxed and the ducks were enmeshed in the net. Sketches of this trap with the net lowered and with it raised are shown in text-figure 26a and b.

Geese were taken by means of a fire at night. They would fly into or near it, and were easily dispatched with clubs.

TAKING OF FISHES

Fishing was very important among the Plains Miwok and those of the lower hills along the courses of the large rivers. Four types of nets were used. A dip net with circular opening and a very long pole was used in the deep holes in the rivers. The seine (yo'ho, P, N) was from six to eight feet wide, was as much as forty feet long, and was usually placed across a river or lagoon where conditions were favorable. Several men drove the fish into the net, where they were either caught by the gills or impounded as the net was drawn ashore. This net was employed for all kinds of fish, including the salmon. In the slack water of the delta region, and especially along rush-bordered rivers and marshes, it was used with the tule balsa, its lower edge weighted with balls of mud wrapped in leaves. No balsa was employed in the swifter waters upstream, and here the seine was rarely used, but was replaced by the set net (yû′gû, P. N; lū′sume, C; la′ssa, C). It was like the seine, but smaller. Its lower edge was fastened securely

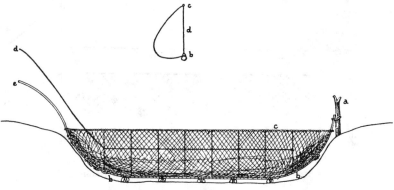

Fig. 27.—Set net for catching fish.

to a wooden bow which in turn was weighted with stones. It was set in a riffle or other advantageous spot and formed a rather deep pocket, across the opening of which several vertical trigger strings were stretched. As the fish passed these strings the signal was conveyed to a watcher on shore by means of a long string, attached to either a cocoon rattle or to the watcher, often about his neck. Upon receiving the signal the watcher pulled up the net, removed the fish, and reset the net. The features of this net are shown in text-figure 27. Sometimes men dove upstream from the net to frighten the fish down to it. A fourth type of net was the casting net (mōla′nna, P). This net had a large circular opening, which automatically spread wide as the net was thrown into the water. It was attached to a long rope and closed itself as it was drawn ashore.

In taking the larger fish, especially the salmon (kosimo, C) and the white salmon (toinoyo, C), the two-pronged harpoon (sīla'nna, P; sī'laa, N; gula'a, C; tco'llo, C) was much used. Its detachable points (sa'tnīpa, C) were made from deer leg bone, and it was of the type common in California. The two detachable points were each secured to the pole by a short, very strong leader of native string, so as to make toggles of them when they come off the prongs, upon being thrust into the fish. The pole was from ten to fifteen feet in length and was made of ash (pa'ñasu, C), *Fraxinus oregona*, or of mountain mahogany (bakilo, C), *Cercocarpus parvifolius*. A three-pronged harpoon was said also to have been used by the Central Miwok.

The sturgeon, found only in Plains Miwok territory, was caught with the hook and line. The "hook" (ya'lūtc, P) was a straight piece of deer bone with both ends sharpened and attached at its middle to the line.[62] A large sucker was used as bait and it was necessary to fish from a balsa. A large sturgeon was able to tow a balsa for a considerable time. It was, therefore, necessary to have a line a quarter of an inch or more in diameter. When the sturgeon ceased towing, it was played until near enough to strike on the head with a special sturgeon club, about eighteen inches in length.

We have no account of fish hooks among the Miwok, yet the Field Museum has a fish worm carrier (70190) from the Southern Miwok of Yosemite valley, perhaps a modern type. This consists of a bottle shaped bundle of sedge *(Cyperus virens)* leaves, within which the worms were confined. It is not a woven container.

Hotca (C) was a spear with obsidian point and mountain mahogany shaft, used solely to spear whitefish in the higher mountains. These were speared in shallow water.

Small fish, such as rainbow trout *(Salmo iridens),* were sometimes caught by hand in the holes along the banks of creeks and rivers.

Informants said that formerly basket traps were used for salmon and other fish, but they had never seen them and could not describe them.

On the Stanislaus river, salmon (kosimo, C) went up as far as Baker's bridge, where there is a waterfall. On the Tuolumne river they went at least as high as La Grange, as did also the white salmon (toinoyo, C). Salmon were caught in the late spring. They worked the sand out of the way with their tails when spawning in shallow water.

---

[62]Cf. Barrett, 1910, pl. 22, fig. 3.

In such positions they were speared. They were caught with nets also in the same season in the Stanislaus river. Most people used the net, as but few understood the spear. A fire built beside the river served as a lure to make spearing easy at night.

The eggs (pu'le, S) of the salmon were used as food. They were dried and preserved for winter use. When needed the dried eggs were soaked in water over night and then boiled for an hour. They might be simply washed and cooked immediately if haste required. When boiled they were eaten with a little salt. The fresh roe was prepared by boiling in a basket.

Lamprey eels were taken in the ordinary fish net, but there was no particular effort made to secure them and there was no special eel net or trap. They were eaten.

An unidentified fish called sununu (C) was described as six to eight inches long and big-headed like a catfish. It was eaten. It could not be caught in a net, and was the only fish shot with bow and arrow by the Central Miwok. Its capture by this method was indulged in only by boys. The arrows employed were wooden pointed. Before shooting the boys called, "Yenene, yenene." The fish was said to make the same sound, though softly, after being removed from the water.

Mashed buckeye nuts *(Æsculus californica)* and soaproot *(Chlorogalum pomeridianum)* were used as fish poisons (huyapna, C), being put in small creeks or pools. The fish, including eels, gradually came to the surface and floated belly up. There was no special method of preparing fish thus killed.

INSECT FOODS AND MEDICINES

Grasshoppers, ko'djo (P, N), añuto (C), ko'tco (C, S), were much esteemed as food and were taken in systematic drives, usually in June. An entire village, or several villages, assembled in an open grassy area, where the insects were abundant. A grassy area, surrounded by a strip of bare ground, was preferred. Each family dug one or more holes, a foot in diameter and three feet deep. These were the focal point of the drive. Quantities of dry grass were piled on the ground among these holes, to be used as a smudge. If available, pine branches were set up for the insects to alight on.

The people then formed a large circle, the diameter depending on the number participating, and drove the grasshoppers toward these pits. Men, women, and children swung bunches of grass back and forth like brooms. The narrowness of the pits contributed greatly to the capture of the insects, making it difficult for them to jump out. When the insects had been corralled in the pits and in the area immediately surrounding them, the dry grass was lighted. This singed the wings of those that tried to fly and smothered most of the remainder. The grasshoppers were in part immediately eaten and in part dried for winter use. In either case they were cooked further. When all was ready the chief of the group would say: "Let us eat and have a good time."

There were two methods of cooking grasshoppers, parching in an openwork basket, and cooking in the earth oven. This oven was circular, twelve to eighteen inches deep, six feet in diameter. A layer of hot stones was put in it. These were covered with green tule (puya, N), then grasshoppers. The grasshoppers were in turn covered with green tule. Hot stones were put on the pile above the tule covering. The cooking took less than half a day. Several families cooked in the same oven. The grasshoppers belonging to each were segregated by layers or partitions of tule. Women made and tended the oven, although sometimes old men dug the pit.

A Northern Miwok informant participated in an unusual drive at Jackson, Amador county. A vineyardist invited the Indians to rid his vines of grasshoppers, paying them in flour, sugar, and other commodities. In the very early morning the old women (grandmothers) beat the vines, so that the grasshoppers fell into burden baskets (dülma, N) held below. Seed-beaters (tcama, N), of second-growth chaparral, were used to knock the insects off. With dew on the leaves the grasshoppers did not fly. The grasshoppers were transferred to acorn-soup baskets (wilûka, N), covered with basket plaques (ulita, N). After scalding, the grasshoppers were spread on basket plaques to dry.

Cocoons from a hairy caterpillar, perhaps the Army Worm, were called lū'lūmai. They were found on bushes, and being brown in color were hard to see. The collectors called the syllable *lul*, which is said to cause them to shake so that they can be seen. Apparently, the vibration of the voice affects them. The chrysalids were steamed in the earth oven, or boiled, and eaten with salt. If the quantity was great, the surplus was sun-dried and stored in twined storage baskets (hupulu,

C). When used later they were soaked in hot water two or three minutes to soften them, then eaten with acorn mush.

Chrysalids of the Pandora Moth, *Coloradia pandora*, (tikku, C), found high in the mountains, were parched.[63]

Five-inch green "worms" (okō'medü, C), found on certain plants yielding edible seeds, were squeezed out, braided in a long rope, and wound around the arm. Later they were steamed. Both men and women gathered them.

The larvae of the yellowjacket, called me'lñayu (C), were also eaten. The finding of the yellowjacket nest involved following a yellowjacket to it. A grasshopper leg was used as bait and a dry pod of *Holcus lanatus* (hesnila, C) was attached to the grasshopper leg. As the yellowjacket flew off with the marked grasshopper leg, it was possible to follow its flight because of the easy visibility of the dry pod.

The raspberry gall (woaiko, C) on the leaves of *Quercus douglasii* is caused by the insect *Dryophanta echina*. Oak galls contain much tannic or gallic acid. These are among our best known styptics and are much used in eye washes.[64] The Central Miwok, at least, used a decoction made from the raspberry gall as a medicine for inflamed eyes (patcaku, C).

MOLLUSKS

At Burns' ferry on the Stanislaus river, people from various places camped to collect river mussels (soponoyu, C). These were cooked by sticking them in the sand, so that they projected, covering them with dry brush, and firing it. River mussels were also obtained high up the north fork of the Tuolumne river. A river mussel or fresh-water clam called yō'loli (P, N) was eaten by the Plains and Northern Miwok. These were slightly larger than the ones used in making shell spoons.

Apparently the only gastropod eaten was a land snail called lōpāti (C) which was taken to stop hemorrhage.

SALT

Salt or salt substitute was derived from three sources: from certain springs, from Mono and other saline lakes east of the Sierra Nevada,

---
[63]Cf. Gifford, 1932, 23.
[64]We are indebted to Dr. E. C. Van Dyke for this information.

and from certain plants. Salt from the first two sources was called ko'īyo (P, N, C) and wi'skoyo (C). Saline springs or ponds were few. Two mentioned were: (1) a deposit about a quarter of a mile southwest of the Central Miwok hamlet of Kotolosaku, near the Stanislaus river, Tuolumne county; and (2) two small holes near Coulterville, Mariposa county. The intense summer heat evaporated the brackish water and left the salt in efflorescent crystals. Salt from this source was even scarcer than that obtained from plants. Salt from saline lakes east of the Sierra Nevada, together with piñon nuts, was brought in summer by the Washo and Mono, to trade with the Miwok for acorns, beads, shells, and baskets.

Saline ashes (pū'tcpūtcū, C) were secured from a species of *Umbelliferae,* called he'mpa (N) and toko'pū (C), obtained in the marshes along the lower course of the San Joaquin river. The grass was piled and burned. The saline constituents accumulated in a hard, glassy cake at the bottom of the fire.[65] The wind soon blew the ashes away and the cake was broken for use. According to one informant the salt was not naturally in the grass itself, but the grass was soaked in brackish water, after which it was burned. This commodity was an article of considerable importance in trade.

What was perhaps another plant from which a salt substitute was obtained was called tauwakti (C). It was of the family *Umbelliferae.* It was dried and burned on clean ground. The ashes were worked with the hand and water on a rock, then eaten with acorn soup.

TOBACCO AND PIPES

The tobaccos *Nicotiana bigelovii*[66] and *Nicotiana attenuata* were smoked. Tobacco was called ka'sü (P, N, C) and kahu (S). In Central and Southern Miwok hū'tīa denoted dry tobacco ground up and ready to smoke. The whole plant was usually gathered about the time the seeds were ripe, and while the leaves were still green. It was dried in the shade and, to make the best grade for smoking, the leaves were broken into fine bits. Before filling the pipe the leaf fragments were further reduced between the hands by rotating one palm upon the other. A poorer grade was made by pulverizing the small stems and refuse. Tobacco was stored and carried in a skin pouch called ya'ūni (P, N). It

---

[65]Cf. Kroeber, 1929, 262.
[66]Setchell, 404.

was smoked in a short, tubular, wooden pipe. Men and boys smoked, but excessive smoking was believed to cause pimples. Women smoked only to cure bad colds. A man who was smoking passed his pipe to a friend who had none. After a few puffs it was returned.

The pipe had two forms, both tubular. One form with a head and bell-shaped opening (plate LVI, figs. 2-4; also Handbook, pl. 30) was called tōpo'kila (P) and paū'mma (N, C, S), and was made of oak, ash, maple root, or manzanita (Field Museum specimens 70186, 70187, 70189). The other form was cylindrical (plate LVI, fig. 1), was called ka'watcu (C, S), and was confined to the Central and Southern Miwok. It was a straight elder tube, three to six inches in length and the diameter of a finger, made by removing the pith from a section of elder limb and then inserting three or four sticks to plug it and form the bottom of the bowl. At the mouth end of the tube the sticks projected about a quarter of an inch, and the tube was whittled thin to make it easier to hold in the mouth. The remaining specimens, 5-12, shown in plate LVI, are Yokuts pipes, quite similar in form and size to those of the Miwok, showing this small tubular pipe is the prevailing type in this section of California.

Tobacco was tamped in the pipe with a twig so as to leave room for a live coal. This was pressed into the tobacco with a small stick until the tobacco ignited thoroughly. The surface of the elder pipe was frequently moistened with saliva, to keep it cool, and rolled between the hands to prevent burning. When the walls became too thin a new pipe was made.

The principal supply of tobacco came from wild tobacco plants, but seeds were, in some cases, planted. This was done about March. Careful growing produced larger leaves and better flavor. Fairly well watered and burnt over ground was selected, preferably on a northern slope. Sometimes an old log was burned and tobacco seeds planted in the ashes. The seeds were scattered and the ground scratched with a stick. Planting was done by old men. No ceremony accompanied planting, harvesting, or use.

Illustrative of the effect of excessive smoking is the anecdote about five "poisoners" (tuyuku, C) who had a contest to determine which could smoke longest. After half a day of smoking in the sunshine they were all overcome by dizziness and sleep.

A decoction of finely powdered tobacco leaves was sometimes drunk as a very effective emetic. Moreover, tobacco and lime were eaten by the Central and Southern Miwok, as well as by the Yokuts. A small stone mortar (wowi, C) was used for pulverizing the mixture of tobacco and calcined shell. The wowi was an ancient mortar, not made by the Miwok for the purpose, but picked up in a creek bed, and supposed to have been made by Coyote. The pestle was called kawatci (C), like pestles in general. The participants sat on the ground in a circle, as when smoking. There was no special posture. Tobacco eating was not connected with ceremonial dances, but was indulged in as a purification. Usually middle-aged or old men and women ate it, not the young people. Apparently the custom was more prevalent among the Southern, than the Central, Miwok. If a company of people had over-indulged at the evening meal to the extent of feeling uncomfortable, one of them said, "Why not pulverize some tobacco?" The tobacco was then pounded in a small mortar. One or two large, long, heavy shell beads, or a piece of abalone, were calcined. After cooling for about fifteen minutes they were pulverized with the tobacco and the mixture moistened with a little water. Then the mixer would say to some man or woman, "Do you want to try some?" The person invited licked off the tobacco and lime adhering to the pestle. Each person might lick the pestle four or five times before he had enough. After a few minutes each arose and went away to vomit. Then he bathed and went home.

VARIOUS ACTIVITIES

FIRE

The fire drill (sosa'nna, P, N; kaia'nna, C, S) consisted of a "hearth" or block, and a rod of well seasoned buckeye wood.[67] Among the Central Miwok of the hills the drill was called kayana, the hearth siwü, and the act of drilling fire, kayana. The drill was rotated between the hands. A hearth and drill are shown in plate LI, fig. 1. The fine, heated dust resulting from the drilling, ran down a small slot on the side of the hearth and collected upon some tinder, tceke (S), which was usually rotten buckeye wood, dry pine needles, shredded cedar

---

[67]One informant stated that the base block was made of cedar while the vertical stick was of elderberry. The Field Museum of Natural History has a Central Miwok specimen (70141) in which both are of cedar (*Libocedrus decurrens*).

bark, or finely shredded grass. Among the Central Miwok of the mountains dry white punk (yeska) from rotten hollow trees was preferred as tinder. In the course of a minute the accumulated heat produced a glowing coal in the dust. This was fanned into flames in the tinder by gentle blowing.

Fire was obtained also by percussion (hulu, C) at least among the Central Miwok. Two sorts of stone, called sitikwina (C) and kolubu (C), were struck together, the sparks being caught on white punk. Sitikwina would seem to be a flint, for it is also used on arrows. Kolubu is perhaps iron pyrites.

Fire wood was obtained from fallen timber when possible. Sometimes a dead tree was felled by burning. The wood was carried either in a bundle tied with a rope or by means of the burden basket.

Haku (C) was a torch of dry pine needles tightly bound with a split withe or twig to a stick. It burned fifteen or twenty minutes, when a fresh bundle of pine needles was attached to the stick. The torch was used especially for night travel.

CARRYING

Baskets of water and acorn soup were carried on the right shoulder, steadied with both hands. No leaves were put on the water to prevent its spilling. Sometimes a basket of water or soup was carried by setting it in a burden basket and carrying it on the back with the aid of the tump line (luke, C) of deer skin. No carrying net was employed. Deer were carried by tying the four legs together with skin slit up from the hoof of each foot. They were carried either on the head or over both shoulders. In the latter case the head of the carrier was slipped through the space between the deer's tied legs and body, the legs being held on the carrier's chest.

The burden basket and the carrying cradle are described under "Basketry". A litter (taka, C) of branches was employed in transporting the corpse to the funeral pyre, and in recent times to the grave. Modern examples are made of boards and have four legs.

CLIMBING

In scaling a straight smooth large tree trunk, a small dead tree was sometimes set against it to serve as a ladder (tcone, C). Another climbing apparatus, called anga (C), consisted of a long pole, in some cases twenty to twenty-four feet, usually of hazel wood, with two crosspieces of hazel wood near the top. These were lashed on with split maple (sayi, C) shoots (from the base of a burnt tree), so as to form two obtuse and two acute angles with the pole. The base of the hazel pole formed the upper part of the apparatus, which was hooked over a limb and used more as a rope than a ladder. The greatest diameter of the pole probably did not exceed an inch and a half. The climber went up it hand over hand with his feet against the trunk. The hazel wood for the anga was cut with a sharp-edged stone (sawa tepeppi, C) naturally fractured and not chipped.

Smaller trees were climbed by putting the arms around them and the soles of the feet against the trunk. The knees were not pressed against the trunk as in the white man's way of shinning up a tree.

In the University's collection is a Southern Miwok wooden hook (1-10332), made from a small tree trunk with the base of a branch projecting from it at a forty-five degree angle, thus making a hook. The handle is slightly over five feet long. This was used to draw limbs to gatherers of pine cones or other tree products, and to hook down dead limbs for firewood. A second example (1-10333) is of about the same length. Both were made with steel tools, but no doubt exemplify an ancient type.

DIGGING

The digging stick (sū'pe, C, S) was three or four feet long and usually made of mountain mahogany, but sometimes of Buck Brush, paiwa (C), *Ceanothus cuneatus*. The piece to be used for a digging stick was hacked off with a sharp-edged stone and scraped with flint. Its point was hardened by fire. It was held in both hands like a quarter staff and jabbed into the ground close to the object to be dug. The left hand grasped the stick eight or ten inches above the point. The right hand grasped it a foot or slightly more above the left hand. Two examples in the Field Museum are 70178 and 70179. An example is shown in plate LIX, fig. 5. For digging bulbs from the sun-baked, hard ground, a digging stick was more effective than a steel spade, for only the minimum quantity of earth was moved.

SHELTER

After food, house materials perhaps reflect the physical environment more than any other feature of Miwok material culture. Miwok structures were of several kinds: (1) the conical dwelling house wholly above the ground, (2) the sun shelter, (3) the semi-subterranean conical dwelling house, (4) the semi-subterranean assembly house, (5) the sudatory or sweat-house, (6) the ceremonial circular structure of brush, (7) the ceremonial rectangular structure of brush, (8) the grinding booth, (9) the acorn granary, and (10) the blind of green boughs from which to shoot birds and mammals.

DWELLINGS

Difficulty was encountered in determining the exact scope of the terms applied to houses, especially since purely aboriginal structures are completely lacking and intermediate types common. Apparently, too, there is considerable doubt in the native mind as to just how the terms were applied formerly. The following seem to be the several types of dwellings:

Umū'tca (P, N, C) seems to be the specific term for a conical bark house, sometimes with an inner layer of pine needles and an outer layer of earth heaped against its lower parts.

Kō'dja (P), and ko'tca (N, C) apparently designate a semi-subterranean earth-covered dwelling.

Ū'tcū (C, S) apparently designates a modern board house.

Wo'lle (P), ko'llī (N), and mole (C) designate a simple conical framework of poles covered with a thatch of brush, grass, or tule (wallakayu, C) bound on, in overlapping courses, with grapevine withes. In the hot, dry, rainless summer, the thatch was put on loosely, so as to allow free passage of air, thus making a shade or sun shelter. The terms also apply to shades or sun shelters more or less rectangular and flat-topped in form. Such easily constructed shades were erected on summer camping trips. The flat-topped shade, in particular, served as a pleasant working or resting place by day, for the women and children, and as a sleeping place by night. Often thistle stems (*Carduus californicus*), sawala (C), were laid about such a sleeping place to keep away rattlesnakes, king snakes, and a large lizard called metubu (C), which was reputed to bite and not let go, thus causing the victim's death and subsequent cremation with the lizard still attached. Her-petologists state that the only reptile to be feared was the Pacific Rattle-snake *(Crotalus oregonus)*.

Tcaama (C) was a portable conical house with tule mat covering and tule mat door. All of the mats were fastened to sticks, for rolling and ready transport. This type was employed below 1500 feet elevation in Central Miwok territory.

Sitcma (C) was a very small conical hut, covered with either bark or tule. An aged person or a newly menstruating girl was relegated to it. Apparently the special designation refers to use rather than to any structural peculiarity.

In the mountains the preferred covering for conical dwellings, which ranged from eight to fifteen feet in diameter, was slabs of Incense Cedar bark (ene'na, N, C, S), but bark from other conifers was also used. This was stripped only from dead trees, and the Digger Pine was especially mentioned for the Upper Sonoran zone, the Western Yellow Pine and Big Tree *(Sequoia gigantea)*, pusine (C), for the Transition zone. No framework or center post was necessary: the bark slabs were leaned together and supported one another. No binding was required. Weather tightness was secured by overlaying the cracks with other slabs until there were three or four thicknesses. The entrance was an opening left in the sloping side. There was no built-out frame-work or doorway. The opening was closed with a large bark slab, kept leaning against the house when not in place. Powers (fig. 37) pictures a half-open summer hut of bark.

Large earth-covered semi-subterranean dwellings, in which a dozen people could live, were constructed at times, in the plains, hills, and mountains. The pit of such a one was examined at the site of the former village of Eyeyaku, near Tuolumne, at about 2500 feet eleva-tion. This type of dwelling was similar in construction, but smaller than, an assembly house (hañi, C), to be described below; it was, how-ever, entered by a ladder through the roof.[68] There was no dancing in this type of house. The Plains Miwok describe this as a rather rare type of winter house, built by men of importance.

In the center of a dwelling was a fireplace, a shallow depression. The fire furnished warmth, and light at night. Here some of the cook-

---

[68]Krause, map 4.

ing was done. Beside the fire was the earth oven, a simple pit a foot or eighteen inches deep by a foot or more across. In it, by means of hot stones, acorn bread, greens, bulbs, corms, meat, and fish, were baked or steamed.

The inmates slept on and under mats or skins (usually deerskins, talka, C) spread upon Digger or Western Yellow Pine needles on the earthen floor. A chief used bear hides for bed and seat. Occasionally a well-to-do man had a sleeping bench (etcī'nnī, P; ya'ña, N) or bed of willow or other poles, raised fifteen to eighteen inches off the floor. Sometimes a small stump or block of wood served as a stool. Leaves of a species of *Cyperus* (kistsi, C) were used for a seat outdoors as well as indoors. Pine needles were piled up for a pillow, or sometimes a rolled coyote (aseli, C) skin was used.

In the dwellings of poor people there might be a scarcity of bed covers, so that a person would have to sleep between fires to keep warm. A man might lie facing the main fire with a small fire of oak bark behind him. Oak bark was selected because the coals retained heat for a long time. The man's back might become purple from the heat.

Only one family occupied a house, though sometimes a newly married son or daughter might reside with the family for a time after marriage. The new relative-in-law did his share in providing for the whole family.

EARTH LODGE

The large, semi-subterranean assembly and dance house (hanē'pū, P; ha'ñī, N, C, S) characteristic of central California, was constructed by the Miwok. It was never used as a dwelling or even as sleeping quarters for the men, except sometimes when a ceremony was being held in the village. It was in charge of an official fire tender (wükü'ppe, P, N). The assembly house was for social and ceremonial gatherings. It was the place where gambling and dancing were conducted. Frequently when people cooked meat or acorns they took some to this house to distribute to other people.

A large pit, forty or fifty feet in diameter, was dug to a depth of three or four feet. Over this was erected a roof in the form of a low cone, supported by heavy beams. These in turn were supported by means of four center posts (to'le, tco'ñe) and eight side posts (text-figure 28).[69] The edges of the cone rested on the edge of the pit. This cone was covered with thatch and earth, which made the roof air and water tight. In having four center posts the structure resembled that of the Southern Maidu,[70] but resembled the Pomo structures in the eight additional posts and octagon of stringers.[71]

One of its chief adjuncts was the large foot drum (tū'mma, P, N); five to ten feet long, made from a section of a log. Various woods were used, though the accidentally hollowed trunk of a white oak was preferred. Further hollowing was by burning. Half of the log, forming a semicircle or less in cross section, was placed over a pit two or three feet deep, between two of the rear posts, and tangent to the rear wall of the house, but within it. The pit served as a resonance chamber, both ends of the drum being left open. The drum was stamped upon, the drummer at times steadying himself by means of an adjacent post. Drums were replaced only when rotten. The space around the drum is called adja (C) and, during ceremonies, is occupied by the singers. The floor where the spectators sat was covered with pine needles or sedge (Carex), kissi (C).

After the timbers for the building had been gathered it took only four or five days to erect the building, everyone in the village helping. The wood used was oak, usually obtained by burning down the trees. If only two or three men were employed in obtaining the timbers, it took them two months.

The first step in the actual construction of the house was the excavation. The size of the area to be excavated was carefully measured. The measure of the radius was called oyisa yaña, literally "four men." Four men actually stretched out on the ground, the head of one man touching the feet of the next man. If we consider the men as averaging five and a half feet, the diameter would be forty-four feet. The excavating was done with digging sticks.

Next the four center posts which supported the roof were put in place, forming the four corners of a square, each side being the reach of a man in length. Four horizontal pieces were tied with withes to the tops of these posts. From these, radial beams were laid sloping to the sides of the pit, but supported midway by an octagon of stringers resting upon the eight side posts. (See diagram, text-figure 28a.) The

---

[69]See also Kroeber, 1925, fig. 39.
[70]Dixon, 1905, fig. 41.
[71]Barrett, 1916, fig. 2.

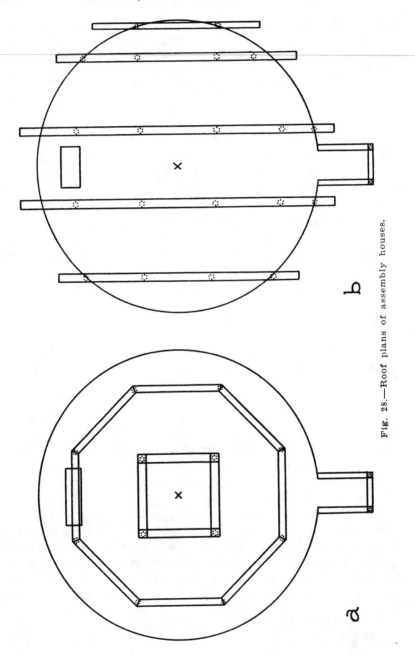

Fig. 28.—Roof plans of assembly houses.

four center posts were each about one foot in diameter, the eight side posts smaller. The stringers were about six inches, the radial roof beams about five inches, and the numerous horizontal closely laid cross sticks upon which the roofing material was laid about three inches, in diameter. The posts were of oak, the stringers and roof beams of buckeye or willow. The four center posts were imbedded two feet, the others one foot. The two rear center posts were treated with "medicine" and only dancers could approach them closely. Posts were either notched or naturally forked at the top to hold the stringers.

A thatch of brush, topped with Digger or Western Yellow Pine needles, never Sugar Pine needles, was next put on. This was followed by the final covering of earth. Altogether the roof was a foot and a half or two feet thick. The opening in the top of the conical roof served as the smoke hole, the fire being built directly under it. The entrance was on any side.

Certain niceties appear in placing brush and earth on the roof. The first layer of brush, which was laid radially over the numerous horizontal roof timbers, was of willow. On this another layer at right angles was placed. The third layer was of a shrub with many close parallel twigs that kept the earth covering from leaking through and resisted rot. The proper depth of the earth layer was four or five inches and was measured by thrusting in the hand. The proper depth came to the base of the thumb.

The digging of the fireplace in the center of a new assembly house took place at the celebration following its completion. A digging stick was the tool; the depth to which dug was about a foot; its diameter between two and three feet.

At Chakachino, a post-Caucasian village near Jamestown, there have been four assembly houses within the memory of the informant, Tom Williams. When one became old and rotten it was torn down, the occasion being one for merrymaking. Also, the death of a chief was followed on one occasion by the burning of the assembly house as a mourning observance, as was the usual Miwok custom. Following the construction of each new assembly house at Chakachino, Miwok from various villages came to the opening ceremonies.

The following notes refer to a semi-subterranean assembly house (plate XXXVIII, figs. 1 and 2; text-figure 28b) at Jackson valley, near Ione, Amador county, in Northern Miwok territory, as it appeared in 1917. It was built in 1913. In 1927 the roof had rotted and was replaced. Only the points in which it differs from the type described above are noted.

Diameter 36 ft. Depth of excavation 3½ ft. to 4¾ ft., depending on slope of ground outside. Door on east side. The south side had been washed out and repaired with a stone wall, and mud mortar, a modern innovation. All of the posts are of white oak and water oak. The stringers are not radially arranged, but extend from front to back, overlapping the edge of the pit, in some cases over three feet. Where stringers overlap over a post they are beveled to make a snug joint, and spiked. The center posts are 8' 8" high, the posts at the walls 4' 6", all others intermediate. The short roof beams across stringers are five to three inches in diameter, in five rows, and total 265 individual pieces. The center row is nine feet wide, the two rows flanking it each eight feet wide, and the two outside rows of varying width owing to the curvature of the side of the pit. This means that the two center lines of posts and stringers are nine feet apart, and the two sides lines each eight feet from these. The smoke hole is at the peak of the roof between the four center posts, as in Maidu assembly houses. The entrance passage is 6' 10" long, 5' 10" high, 5' 6" wide, and brush and earth-covered. It is closed by a modern, hinged, board door.

At Big Creek near Groveland two pits encircled by rings of earth indicate two former assembly houses. The present circular assembly house[72] is the modern wooden substitute, without excavated floor and earth covering. It is called tapla utcu (C). The inside diameter is thirty and one-half feet. The main radial rafters divide the roof into five sectors. These are crossed by five concentric sets of stringers resting on posts. A sloping ladder runs up the roof to a small platform, from which the chief or orator addressed the people.

No evidence was obtained among the Miwok to indicate that the smoke hole formerly was used as an entrance, or that the side entrance developed from an original draft opening. Whether this negative evidence means that this type of house reached the Miwok only after the smoke hole entrance had gone out of use, or whether the evolution of the features mentioned occurred too early to be remembered, we are unable to decide.

The distribution of semi-subterranean earth-covered houses is wide,

---

[72]For view of this assembly house, see Dorsey, 214.

but only in California is the foot drum employed as an adjunct of the house in its ceremonial form. It seems likely that the original diffusion of the house to central California was as a dwelling. With its adaptation to the needs of the god-impersonating cult, came the introduction of the foot drum and the attribution of sanctity to certain of the posts of the house. Whether the foot drum is a central Californian invention or an importation from elsewhere is not evident. However, the possible connection of the pit and foot drum with the *sipapu* pit and board covering of the Hopi kiva suggests itself.

SWEAT-HOUSE

The sweat-house (tcapu'ya. C, S) was not slept in, was not an habitual club, and was not used as a lounging place for men and boys. It was only a sudatory for men, for hunting and curative purposes, heated by fire and not by steam. It was a conical,[73] earth-covered structure, six to fifteen feet in diameter and of a height permitting only half erect posture. The largest would accommodate ten men. The house was built over a pit two or three feet deep. Brush, Digger or Western Yellow Pine needles, bark (in the mountains cedar bark), and earth formed the successive layers of the roof. The smoke hole at the top was about six inches in diameter.

Each man who sweated had a little pile of wood to feed the fire. Whoever added most fuel, thus creating most heat, was regarded as the strongest. The fire was preferably of white oak. Often several men would sweat for two hours, then yield their places to a second group. Each man knelt and put his face on the ground, so as not to be smothered.

A deer hunter entered the sweat-house before sunrise and stayed from one to three hours. Then he jumped into a pool in the creek. He repeated the sweating and bathing once or twice, continuing until about 1 p. m. This was thought to purify him. Sometimes a man on leaving the sweat-house would faint before he reached the creek. Some men sweated before dancing, so as to "feel better" when dancing.

The sweat-house was used especially by men who had bad luck in deer hunting. It was supposed to make their legs strong, so that they could walk far without aching. The sick were not sucked in the sweat-

---

[73]Powers (fig. 34) pictures a domed structure.

house, but were simply sweated there. The sweat-house did not enter into shamanistic treatment.

When a chief announced a social or ceremonial gathering many men sweated to be successful in killing deer for the celebration. If a man was not sweated he would not get deer. Sweating was not necessary for rabbit hunting or mountain lion hunting.

It seems likely that the sweat-house was more regularly used for deer-hunt preparations than for curative purposes. However, men with rheumatism and headache, at least, made use of it. They sweated two or three hours, then bathed in a pool. The legs were also scratched with a sharp quartz crystal as a curative measure. Sometimes, in frosty weather, a family with a poor house would occupy the sweat-house.

BRUSH ASSEMBLY HOUSE

The circular brush assembly house, usually roofed with brush and pine needles, but without earth covering, was used in summer for mourning ceremonies. In the winter these were held in the semi-subterranean assembly house. The name of the brush assembly house varied locally; at Jamestown it was lutcumte (C), north of the Stanislaus river it was tewate (C). At West Point it was kütca (N), and among the Southern Miwok it was sala. It was not ordinarily used for dances like kuksuyu, although this dance was once held in one at Knights Ferry. In July, 1927, a roofless example thirty feet in diameter, was seen at Chakachino, near Jamestown, Tuolumne county. It had been constructed some months before to hold the mourning ceremonies for a deceased resident of that place.

The brush assembly house was much smaller than the semi-subterranean assembly house, and measured only two and one-half men (otega yaña homotani) in radius. The short men were used as measures at that. They lay down on the ground as for measuring the larger ceremonial structure. The "half" was measured by a third man lying on his back doubled up. The openwork nature of this structure allowed the breezes to blow through it.

Many of the ancient brush houses were rectangular, flat topped, and erected on the surface of the ground without excavation. These were designated as kutcala (C). There were large doorways on two opposite sides, with smaller doorways on the other two sides. The roof and sides were formed of green boughs. There was one center post, four corner posts, and one post in the middle of each side. This type of building, coupled with its use for mourning ceremonies, suggests a southern Californian derivation. It was erected by four or five men at the behest of the chief, who fed the builders. The chief's wife cooked for them. Ownership appears to have been vested in the chief and these men.

GRINDING HOUSE

A small conical grinding or milling house of bark slabs or brush might be built over a bedrock mortar or an imbedded portable mortar as protection from sun and bad weather. The one shown in plate XXX, fig. 2, was at Railroad flat, Calaveras county. It was made almost entirely of modern boards, with a few cedar bark slabs added. It was six feet in diameter by seven feet in height. Its framework was six poles, each about four inches in diameter at the base. A simple grinding shelter was sometimes made of stones and brush. This served as a partial sun shade and windbreak. The grinding house seems to be merely a sun shelter applied to one specific purpose.

ACORN GRANARY

Acorns were stored whole in specially constructed caches. Large ones (tca'kka, P, N, C, S) are shown in plate XXXI, fig. 8. A small one (he'sma, N), built in a low branching bush, was more or less of a makeshift. It was an inverted cone about three and a half feet high, and had a capacity of perhaps a bushel. Powers[74] figures Miwok acorn granaries of the large type.

The large type of cache was constructed with care. Several vertical posts were set firmly into the ground. About these, heavy grapevine or other withes were bound to form hoops. Inside were bound small vertical poles forming the ribs of the cache. Within these was placed a horizontal layer of twigs and brush, inside of which was laid a lining of weeds and grass. So tightly were these caches built, that they were used for the storage of grass seeds. There was no true weaving, but the inside of such a cache resembled a bird's nest in construction.

The smaller of the two illustrated in plate XXXI, fig. 8, stood originally about six feet high. It had four grapevine hoops and a thick roof of weeds and twigs. The larger was nearly twelve feet high, had

---

[74]Powers, fig. 32.

six vertical posts and five grapevine hoops. The conical bottom rested on a block of wood about a foot high by fifteen inches in diameter. Two grapevine hoops passed around an adjacent pine tree, which served as a support for both these caches. The larger cache was five feet in diameter and its conical bottom was about three and a half feet deep. Sometimes the bottom of such a cache was suspended two or three feet off the ground. The top of the cache was covered with layers of grass and brush so placed as to shed the rain. Over this was usually placed a final roof of cedar-bark or pine-bark slabs. Thus was produced a water-tight storehouse where a whole winter's supply of acorns or seeds could be kept. Nearly every family had at least one of these caches, and a man of importance who must provide for feasts required several.

No special opening was provided for removing the acorns or seeds. The construction made it possible to make a rent in the side from which the acorns would run into a basket held below. When a sufficient quantity had been secured, the weeds and grass of the side were readjusted to make it tight again.

According to Powers[75] acorn granaries were sometimes miles from the villages where their owners dwelt.

ARTS AND INDUSTRIES

MORTARS AND PESTLES

For pulverizing food the characteristic stone implements were the bedrock mortar (tco'se, P, N, C, S) and the cobblestone pestle (hō'pa, P; kawa'tcī, N, C. S). Plate XXIX, fig. 2, and Kroeber's Handbook, plate 45a, show mortars in level granite outcrops.

The bedrock mortar was at first a slight natural depression in a granite boulder. With the wear of the pestle a cup (tcose, C, S) was formed. When a cup became too deep, a new one was started a few inches or a few feet away. Such a boulder served as the communal milling place for all the women of a hamlet. Deep mortar holes were used for the preparation of manzanita berries, oats, and other seeds, especially when it was desired merely to crack the shells and not to crush the meats, previous to winnowing. In such a case the pestle was used lightly and also worked sidewise in the hole.

Unworked stones of convenient size and shape served as pestles.

[75]Powers, 351.

These were found in large numbers in the beds of the many mountain streams of the region. Examples are shown in plate XXXIII, figs. 1-6.

With the bedrock mortar no basketry or other hopper was employed. Consequently, the meal, as it was pounded, spread out over the surface of the rock, and particles often flew over a radius of two or three feet. To collect these particles and to keep the meal heaped about the grinding cup, a soaproot brush (caka'ni, P, N), plate XXXVI, was used at frequent intervals.

When no convenient bedrock mortar was at hand, a flat stone, sufficiently small to be portable, was placed in the floor of the dwelling or grinding house (plate XXX, fig. 2). Such a mortar was called ütü'we (P), ülü'we (N), ū'mme (C, S), tē'sa (C). Holmes shows two such at a mealing place.[76]

Of less importance was the globose, portable mortar, called ü'mme (P, N), wowi and ho'līsu (C), kūyo'pa (S). The Miwok made no portable mortars whatever. All in their possession have been found by them and are said to have been made by Coyote, a supernatural being, who scratched them out or made them sexually. Small portable mortars are shown in plates XXXIV and XXXV, figs. 1-3, and Holmes pictures some.[77] The larger were used for grinding dried meats and fish, especially for old people whose teeth were poor, and for making some kinds of seed meal. Small mortars of this type were employed in grinding medicines and paints. The pestle for such a mortar is called kiwapula (C). With these mortars were used small, carefully shaped pestles (plate XXXII, figs. 5, 7, 8, 10).

Two Northern Miwok mortars, 1-10011 and 1-10504 in the University collection, one of which (1-10011) is illustrated in plate XXXV, fig. 3, show double use. They are small, irregularly shaped meat and nut mortars. On their bottoms are little depressions upon which acorns were held when cracked.

Wooden mortars (umme, C) were said to have been made by the Central Miwok. In them were used stone pestles.

METATES

The metate (kowasila, C) is rare (plate XXXV, figs. 4 and 5), and probably borrowed from the neighboring tribes to the east or southeast.

---

[76]Holmes, 1902, 172, pl. 13.
[77]Holmes, 1902, pl. 9.

There a special muller was used, but among the Miwok the side of a small cobblestone pestle served. When so used it was called hoku (C). The metate may be of recent intrusion, since aged Central Miwok informants denied its presence and no account of food preparation makes any mention of its use, except that published by Holmes.[78]   Metates were among the auriferous gravel finds,[79] so that as early as 1860 they had already been introduced among the Miwok, possibly by Indian miners from east of the Sierra Nevada.

HAMMERS, ANVILS AND COOKING STONES

The uses of the acorn cracker (plate XXXII, fig. 6), called lŭ'pû (P, N, C) and pasákkila (S), with its stone anvil, called ülü'we (P), ü'mme (N), tū'ka (C), and mū'laa (S), have already been outlined in speaking of vegetal foods.

Similarly the uses of the cooking stones (plate XXXII, figs. 1-4) have been described in speaking of the cooking of acorns and other foods.

A flattish, more or less rounded piece of stone was used as an anvil upon which to crack acorns. It usually had a slight, roughened depression on one or both of its flat surfaces, very likely to prevent the acorn from slipping when struck with the hammerstone. Anvils usually were not of steatite, which was apparently too soft and too readily cracked. A small mortar (University collection 1-10504) from Railroad flat, Calaveras county, has four cuppings on its bottom to serve as bases for cracking acorns.

WOODEN BOWLS AND POTTERY

Oaken bowls were commonly made by the Western Mono, but seem to have been rare among the Miwok. The Field Museum of Natural History possesses two, both (70037, 70055) made from the burls of *Quercus kelloggii*. The latter is unfinished and was used as a cider bowl or trencher. The first is a Central Miwok piece, the second a Southern piece.

Tools for making these bowls are described under the caption "Bone and Antler Implements". It seem likely that the manufacture of these

[78]1902, 172, pl. 11.
[79]Holmes, 1901, pl. 3.

bowls was restricted to the Southern Miwok and rare there.   They probably learned the art from their Western Mono neighbors.

Pottery vessels were made by the southerly Western Mono and their Yokuts neighbors, but not by the Miwok.   The nearest approach to pottery among the Miwok is four clay figures of animals in the Field Museum (70278, 1-4), collected by J. W. Hudson in 1901, from the Southern Miwok of the Chowchilla river.   Whether these represent a step in the direction of pottery manufacture or whether they are due to Caucasian example is not known.

STEATITE

Steatite quarries were probably fairly common in Miwok territory, judging from the distribution of steatite, given in "Minerals of California."[80]   There is a stratum of steatite (pukia, C) at the same level in both the south and north walls of the canyon of the north fork of the Tuolumne river.   The latter deposit is about a mile from the outskirts of the town of Tuolumne and is cut by the old Duckwall road.   A spring close by is called Indian spring by Americans, Kolakota by the Miwok. The soapstone quarry itself is called Lotowayaka.   The quarry on the south side of the canyon is called Tile by the Miwok.

Cooking stones for use in baskets were often of steatite.   Steatite vessels, about eight inches in diameter, were used to cook in, being put on the fire.   They were also used as general receptacles.   A poorly formed specimen is shown in plate XXXII, fig. 9.   The Field Museum of Natural History possesses two bowls (70065, 70066) of red steatite, found in 1863 in an ancient cave near Tuolumne.   The second was said to have been used latterly as a grizzly bear charm.   A third Field Museum specimen is 70068 from the Southern Miwok at Ahwahnee.

Powdered steatite was used on babies to relieve chafing under the arms and between the legs.   It was not used for adults.

CHIPPED STONE IMPLEMENTS

The scant information concerning points and blades of flint and obsidian was probably due to the sudden influx of steel implements sweeping them out of use by 1850.   However, a few flint and obsidian pieces have been collected at aboriginal sites in the Sierra Nevada. There is reason to believe that these objects are of Miwok origin.   They

---

[80]Eakle, 217-219.

are illustrated in plate XXXVII. The wealth of flint and obsidian implements from the Plains Miwok territory is described and figured by Schenck and Dawson.

The simplest stone knife was a naturally fractured stone, unworked, such as was used to hack off hazel branches or to cut off maple shoots. A flake of gray "flint" (kolubu, C), unworked, was used to scrape split maple shoots for basketry, and a similar black obsidian flake to scrape down a bow. Luka (C) is the term for a scraper, applied also to steel blades so used. The stone flakes were struck from a core.

A knife (kike, C) of obsidian (sītcan, P; sītcánû, N; pasakka, C) would appear to have been a worked implement. Flint (hágü, P, N; sitikwina, C) and jasper appear not to have been used for knives, except among the Southern Miwok. Mr. W. H. Edwards of Vacaville, California, has a large number of flint blades and points collected from an archaeological site at Merced Falls in Southern Miwok territory. Probably some of these were knives.

A stone saw was used to cut abalone shell, but perhaps it was more in the nature of a file than a saw. The Field Museum of Natural History has an obsidian flake (70183), with greatest dimension twenty-seven millimeters, which was used at Groveland as a scarifier, in sickness and grief.

What is labeled as a hide scraper of chert, from Tuolumne, in Central Miwok territory, is in the Field Museum collection (70180). There are two other Central Miwok examples from Sonora (70161, 70162), both flattish, oval stones, and one of chalcedony from Tuolumne (70163).

A crude, though probably effective, spear was made by binding with sinew a large obsidian or flint spearhead to the end of a smooth mountain mahogany pole about seven feet long. The chief use of the spear was in war. Whether this is the hotca (C) spear described under "Taking of Fishes" is not clear.

In the Field Museum of Natural History there is a six-foot spear (70266) with a brown flint point. The point is a broad equilateral triangle, 30 mm. wide, lashed to the shaft with sinew and some adhesive, perhaps pine pitch. The handle is of hard wood. The basal end of the handle is somewhat pointed, apparently with a steel tool.

ARROW STRAIGHTENERS AND SMOOTHERS

Two well-known types of arrow straighteners were employed, a perforated one of wood (plate LX, fig. 4) or stone and one of grooved stone. Both were called lipippa (C). The perforated type was of manzanita, maple, or stone (Field Museum 70156, Central Miwok). It had a circular hole, not perfectly straight, but with a slight angle at the middle, through which the arrow was thrust and bent after having been warmed over a fire. The stone arrow straightener was of steatite, about the size of one's fist. The transverse groove in it had a slight bend, thus giving an angle against which to bend the arrow. One aged informant possessed one which she had found some years before at Lowönunu (Long Gulch, Tuolumne county), an old camp site.

The Field Museum of Natural History possesses a third type of implement, composed of two opposing, longitudinally grooved sections of pumice (70157, 1-2), described as an arrow shaft plane. This tool is from the Central Miwok.

PROBLEMATICAL STONE OBJECTS

Three of the archaeological objects called "charmstones" and some examples of the obsidian "Stockton curves" were shown to Central Miwok. The "Stockton curves" were declared to be imitation bear claws (tisus uzumatiñ, C) worn on the left hand by dancers of the uzumati or grizzly bear dance. Four of these curves were attached to sticks and these in turn lashed to the four fingers.

The informants said that the charmstones (lepipa, C) were made by the supernatural being, Coyote. One informant declared that a long, slender, double tapered charmstone (kayana, C) was a fire drill to be used in a buckeye "hearth." A very globose charmstone (lakuna, C) she said was used to rub deer skins. A charmstone (hikani, C) with a perforation at one end she declared was used in spinning. We suspect that these attributed uses were only guesses on the part of the informant.

The Field Museum has an obsidian blade labeled a charmstone (70279). It was worn pendent on the chest by a neck loop.

BONE AND ANTLER IMPLEMENTS

The commonest bone implement was the awl (lu'ya, P; tci'lla, N, C; tcu'lla, C), used especially in the manufacture of coiled basketry. A series of awls is depicted in plate XXXIX. These were made chiefly from the splint bone of the deer and from the proximal end of the posterior cannon bone (fused metatarsals). The Field Museum of Natural History possesses an eyed bone needle (70170), 133 mm. long, from the Southern Miwok, and from the Central Miwok a dagger (70264) of a flat piece of elk antler, attached to a leather wrist thong. The dagger is 268 mm. long.

Whistles employed in certain ceremonial dances were made of hollow bones. Jackrabbit and Sierra grouse limb bones were utilized. For examples, see plate LVII, figs. 1–8.

Points of antler were used in the knapping of flint and obsidian points and blades. The Field Museum of Natural History has a Central Miwok knapper set (70146, 1–2), with a guard of buckskin. That institution also has a chisel of deer antler (70154) and a pointed tool of deer antler (70153), both used for picking or digging out wooden bowls, and both Southern Miwok.

Plate LVIII, fig. 11, shows a deer antler implement used for extracting acorns stored by woodpeckers.

Scrapers (otcati, C) of split deer leg bone were used to work down a bow. A sharp tibia was used as a scraper (lutaa, C) to remove hair from a deer hide.

Certain pieces of stone are reputed to be whetstones for bone awls and bone daggers. The best example seen is a slate specimen (70265) in the Field Museum. It was found with the bone dagger (70264) in a cave at Little Tuolumne, in the mountains of the Central Miwok territory. Two other slate examples from the Central Miwok of Tuolumne county are 70164, 1–2.

SOAPROOT BRUSH

The soaproot brush, caka'nī (N), was a hair brush, a scrubber for cooking baskets, and a mealing implement. It was made of fibers from the dry, outer layers of the soaproot *(Chlorogalum pomeridianum)*, palawi (C), laid so that the natural curvature of their bases nested. They were bound temporarily with a withe (plate XXXVI, fig. 1), and the loose upper ends wrapped with a string to produce a handle (plate XXXVI fig 3). The inner part of the soaproot bulb was then scraped to make a mucilaginous dressing which was thoroughly worked into the handle. Upon exposure to the sun and air for a day or two this became very hard. Sometimes pine pitch was used instead of the soaproot juice. Plate XXXVI, fig. 4, shows one of these newly made soaproot brushes, while figures 5 and 7 of this same plate show examples of these brushes which have been so much used that they are worn down. Figures 2 and 6 are good examples of the soaproot brush in prime condition.

WEAPONS

The weapons employed in fighting were the bow and arrow, and the spear. Neither shields nor armor were used. The warrior depended for safety upon dodging the missiles of the enemy. One member of each band of warriors was engaged behind the fighting line, collecting the arrows shot by the enemy. These were shot back at the enemy.

The costume of a warrior consisted of a simple breech clout, a fur foreheadband to keep the long hair in place, and a special cap of grass, very similar to the hunting cap. No moccasins were worn.

THE BOW

The principal weapon for hunting and also for war was the bow and arrow. The bow, called tanúka (P), kútca (N, C, S), oñili (C), and yáwe (S), was fairly heavy, about three feet in length, and about two inches in width at its broadest part. The outer curve of its cross-section was about 90 degrees. It was usually made of spruce or incense cedar and was often reinforced with a fairly heavy backing of sinew. According to Powers,[81] "all the dwellers on the plains, and as far up as the cedar-line, bought all their bows and many of their arrows from the upper mountaineers. An Indian is ten days in making a bow, and it is valued at $3, $4, and $5, according to the workmanship; an arrow at 12½ cents."

However, at Knights Ferry, on the Stanislaus river, the sinew-backed bow was made from the ash tree *(Fraxinus oregana)*, pa'ñasu.

In the mountains of the Central Miwok territory a cedar bough selected for the bow was hacked from the tree and roughly trimmed down with a sharp-edged stone. Then it was worked down by scraping

---

[81]Powers, 352.

with a flake of black obsidian, or a split deer leg bone, and rubbing with a stone "like emery" (paaya, C) and with a piece of scouring rush, *Equisetum arvense* (sakayu, C). The stone was also used for filing the nocks in the bow.

The bow was bent into shape when green, by warming it over the fire. After four or five days of seasoning, deer sinew was applied to the back of the bow. The sinew had been dried on some previous occasion and was now chewed to soften it. It was applied with the fibers running lengthwise of the bow. It was applied in thin layers, pasted on with soaproot juice. A small soaproot, called wolone (C), was roasted, dipped in water, and rubbed over each layer of dried sinew on the back of the bow, giving it a water-tight sealing.

The bow string (tumappa, C) was of twisted milkweed (tumuka, C) fiber, or of sinew. A section about two inches in length, about six inches from the upper end, was wrapped with a half-inch strip of beaver, otter (mesu, C), or other fur, hair side out. This served to deaden the twang of the bow string. Around the center of the bow string was wound a half-inch strip of otter fur, hair side out, lashed securely with deer sinew. This was believed to make a better hold for the nock of the arrow. Perhaps, too, it served to cushion the wrist against the snap of the bow string.

A bow without sinew back was sometimes made for bird killing. Each man usually had one bow, but not every man made his own. The maker of bows was also the maker of arrows. The arrow-release was of the primary type and the bow was held vertically.

The bow, illustrated in plate LIX, fig 1, from Calaveras county, is heavily backed with sinew. The wooden tips are completely covered with it, the sinew of the back of the bow being brought onto the belly side of each tip. Apparently the recurved ends of the nocks are of sinew only, which has become very hard and, at the base of the nock, successfully resists the pull of the bowstring. The sinew at the tip of each nock is folded so as to expose no end. In fact, nowhere on the back is a loose end of sinew visible. The sinew on the back has the appearance of the bark of a tree or shrub. At the center of the bow is a wrapping of a narrow strip of buckskin which passes around the bow thirty times. The bowstring is of three-ply sinew cord. In plate LIX, fig. 1, the bow is shown in reverse. A careful scrutiny of the picture reveals the boundary of sinew and wood along the edge.

A similar bow (70242) was seen in the Field Museum of Natural History with the bowstring of three-ply sinew cord split into two three-ply smaller cords to form a half hitch around each nock.

Bow 50.6439 in the American Museum of Natural History is from a "Calaveras county chief." It is similar to the two discussed in the paragraph above. It is figured and its type discussed by Dixon.[82]

Another bow (70241), in the Field Museum of Natural History, is unfinished. It is broader and flatter than those described above. The nocks are very angular and have the appearance of ⌐⌐ . Some sinew has been laid on the back of the bow and lashed in place•with a cord.

A simple bow with plant fiber bowstring is 70246 in the Field Museum of Natural History collection. Another bow (70240) is in process of manufacture, having been roughly shaped out of a limb of cedar *(Libocedrus decurrens)*. It is from Yosemite valley.

ARROWS

The arrow (ha'ūlo, P; ya'tci, N, C; mu'tckūlū, C, S) used for ordinary hunting purposes, consisted of a simple wooden shaft (pa'ipū, C), with the arrowhead (kī'tce, C) attached directly to it with sinew lashings. The war arrow, also used for big game, was made with a foreshaft (toke', C). The shaft was of the young shoot of a tree, called gilme (P, N), which closely resembles the willow; or young shoots of the Western Sweet-scented Shrub, *Calycanthus occidentalis* (*so'ksokoтu, C*) ; or, apparently of elder. After removing the bark the arrow maker carefully scraped and trimmed the shaft to an even size. Then it was straightened by heating such places as required bending. The shaft was smoothed and polished with a piece of sandpaper-like scouring rush *(Equisetum arvense)*. The foreshaft was made of white oak or of greasewood (lī'mme, C). Like the main shaft it was straightened by means of heat. It was attached to the main shaft with an adhesive which the heat of the animal's body would quickly loosen, so that it would remain in the body, if the main shaft were pulled out or broken off.

The arrowhead, usually of obsidian (pasakka, C) sometimes of flint, was attached directly to the end of the shaft or to the short foreshaft.

---

[82] 1907, 438, fig. 107.

In either case it was fitted into a slot and secured with a sinew wrapping and pitch, the wrapping passing through two side notches in the arrowhead. Informants stated that the arrowhead was sometimes poisoned with a mixture of native salt and deer blood. The efficacy of this "poison" (losa, C) seems doubtful, and it seems not unlikely that some virulent poison, like that of the rattlesnake, may have been employed. The obsidian or flint was flaked from a core by striking it with a hammerstone. The flake was then roughly chipped with a large antler chipping implement (sītca'ia, C; sītca'a, S). The finer chipping, as of notches. was done with a small antler implement (tʉka'wa, S). These antler implements were not mounted in handles. They were simply heated and bound to sticks in order to straighten them, after which they were taken off and used directly in the hand. The material for the arrowhead was grasped in the palm of the left hand, which was protected by a buckskin pad (hesū'pa, C; he'sūmma, S), held in place by the pressure of the fingers on the arrowhead. The Central Miwok said their obsidian came from a high mountain called Kilili, whence it was brought in burden baskets.

The base of the arrow was notched, painted red, and fitted with feathers (sa'li, P, N; ca'la, C), usually of the Western Red-tail Hawk (sūī'yō, P, N; suyu, C). Informants stated that each feather was split down the middle and four half feathers applied to each arrow. (All specimens seen in museums have but three half feathers.) Sinew was chewed to serve as wrapping and binding material. The ends of the half feathers toward the middle of the arrow were lashed on first. The chewed sinew was held in the mouth throughout the operation. The end of the sinew fibers was applied to the arrow with the fingers. Then the shaft was revolved in front of the mouth and the sinew fed out of the mouth as fast as it was wound around the shaft and feathers. Usually about ten arrows were made at a time. On each of these the feathers were fastened at the ends nearest the middle of the shaft, and then the arrow was carefully stood aside. All ten were thus treated before the attachment of the ends of the feathers toward the base. Then the arrowmaker began with the first and fastened the basal ends of the feathers of each with sinew. The feathers were thus lashed on after the arrows had been equipped with stone points. The feathers of the roadrunner, *Geococcyx californicus* (uiuyu, C), were regarded as fine for arrows. Arrows so equipped were believed to always kill deer. Evidently there was a magical connection between the swiftness of the bird on foot and the killing qualities of arrows equipped with its feathers.

Arrows were made by a specialist. Others bought their arrows from him, paying in beads. No property marks or other decorations were used on arrows.

The three arrows shown in plate LIX, figs. 2–4, are of wood with a pithy center, probably elder, and have no foreshaft. The base of the shaft of each has small encircling grooves for the entire distance covered by the hawk feathers. The grooves are most prominent in figure 2. The bases are painted in encircling bands of red, white, and black. Three half feathers are lashed to the base of each arrow with sinew, being bound perfectly flat without folding at either end. Each feather was split up the middle of its quill, and the half feather trimmed to about eight millimeters in width. Figure 2 still has an obsidian point lashed in place with sinew which passes through the two side notches in the obsidian point. On the shaft the holding power of the sinew is increased by encircling grooves in the wood over which it is wound. The other two arrows (figures 3 and 4) lack this grooving. They are now minus points, but have their distal portions painted red. At the proximal end of the red portion there is sinew winding, as though a foreshaft were inserted at that point.

QUIVERS

Two types of quivers were used by the Central Miwok. One, called hononga, was a buckskin bag, kept at home. The other, a carrying quiver called suta, was a cylinder, open at both ends and comprised the entire skin of an animal, minus head and feet, and hair side out. The skin of the black fox or otter was especially valued, but after Americans came dog skins were used. In preparing a skin, it was sewed up the belly where cut for skinning. The tail was left as a pendent ornament. The skin edges where head and feet were cut off were decorated with abalone bangles. No stick or hoop was put in the neck to keep it open, but it was dried with an annular opening.

The carrying quiver had no shoulder strap for suspension, but was carried horizontally in the hand. The arrows were tied in a bundle with buckskin thongs. The bow was carried separately. When the bearer was shooting, either in hunting or warfare, he held the quiver under his left arm so that the arrows could be readily withdrawn.

In the dwelling house was a forked stick projecting upward from the wall. On this was laid the buckskin bag (hononga) in which the arrows were stored. This quiver was closed at one end and unornamented. It had no padding to protect the arrows, but was always kept in a horizontal position. The carrying quiver was usually placed on top of it, after the arrows had been transferred.

A badger skin (1–10230, University collection) folded over a stick, in imitation of a quiver, was carried by the master of ceremonies in a dance held in Yosemite in 1905.

LOOPED STIRRERS AND PADDLES

The University's collection contains four looped mush stirrers, two of oak, two of unidentified material. Three are Southern Miwok, one Central, none Northern nor Plains. Of mush paddles there are nine, three of oak, one of manzanita, five of unidentified wood. Four are Northern Miwok, five Central, and none Southern or Plains. See plate XXXI, figs. 1–5.

A paddle of oak (70104), two of manzanita (70103, 70108), and one of pine (70105), all from the Central Miwok, were seen in the Field Museum of Natural History. 70104 and 70103 were 68 cm. long, 70105 was 79 cm. long. The last had a very narrow blade of only five centimeters width. The Field Museum has also a looped stirrer of hazel (70107) from Groveland, and one of an unidentified wood (70106) from Madera county.

The paddle was the preferred Northern implement, the looped stirrer the preferred Southern implement.

CLOTHING

Children wore no clothing until about ten years of age. The man's clothing, when any was worn, consisted ordinarily of a simple breech clout (taplawū', N) of buckskin which passed between the legs and hung from a buckskin girdle (patca, lūтa, C) as a short apron at the front and back.

The woman's dress[83] consisted, in the north, of a buckskin skirt

---

[83]Powers (p. 348) states that "both sexes and all ages went absolutely naked."

(hū'te, N), which was a simple sarong-like wrapping about the loins. It reached to about half way between the knees and the ankles and had a fringe several inches in length. In addition to this dress and an oblique band of buckskin across each shoulder, the Central Miwok used more commonly a two-piece dress. The rear one (se'kī, C) was donned first. The front dress or apron (he'ssa, C) was then put on to overlap the two edges of the back dress. The Central Miwok also wore two-piece grass skirts reaching from the waist to the knees, and in suitable localities skirts (poso'wan, P) were made of shredded tule. Under the skirt the women wore a buckskin clout almost identical to that worn by the men, but called he'tta (N). Cedar bark was not used for skirts. No basket caps were worn.

When the weather required both sexes wore blankets. These were made from dressed skins of various animals: deer, bear, mountain lion, coyote, and others. Buffalo skins were sometimes used. These were obtained by trade from the Washo and Eastern Mono.[84] Mo'a (C) was a blanket of two or more sewed deerskins. The commonest blanket, however, was made by winding narrow strips of rabbit skin about cords and weaving these, using plain cord as woof, into a loose but very warm blanket (plate LXI). It was called ūdjū'le (P), yū'ptī (N, C, S). All blankets, particularly of rabbit skin, were used especially as bed covers, but served as garments in cold weather. Except for rabbit skin blankets made in the low foothill region, the Miwok imported most of theirs from the Washo in the north and the Eastern Mono in the south.

A rare type of blanket (le'ka, P; to'nnī, N) was made of duck or goose feathers. The individual feathers were bound to a central cord by a smaller wrapping cord, thus producing a feather rope. Such strands formed the warp for a blanket similar to the rabbit skin robe. It was used almost entirely as an outer garment, but not subjected to rough usage. It was rarely seen in the mountains.

No feather skirt was worn by the Miwok, except the ceremonial one elsewhere described.

A much prized feather belt, ya'yame (N), was worn as a decoration and used as a medium of exchange. The Central Miwok made belts of California woodpecker (palatada, C) scalps, sewed on a buckskin belt and fringed with olive shell disks (tunni, C). Such belts were

---

[84]For discussion of western occurrences of buffalo, see Merriam, 1926.

worn by rich men, their wives, and daughters. Also, belts (tē'pa, P, N; lü'taiya, N; lu'ta, C) were made of shell beads.

Ordinarily no foot covering was worn, but moccasins (solo'me, P, N; mamko, C) were used in cold weather and for journeys in very rough country. The moccasin was a one-piece affair of buckskin, lined with shredded cedar bark. There was a seam up the heel and up the front of the moccasin, sewed with milkweed fiber thread. Overlapping pieces were bound around the ankle. The moccasins were made by men, though worn by both sexes. The examples in plate LXII, figs. 1 and 2, are of Washo origin, but illustrate the Miwok type. They give evidence of having had an outer heel and sole sewed to the bottom. The top flaps have been cut away.

THE HAIR

Adults wore the hair long, sometimes to the waist. It was allowed to flow loosely, was made into a simple knot, or was gathered into a bunch at the back of the head, being tied at the neck with a string called weka (C). It was not only tied, but doubled back on the head, in hot weather or when hunting. It was never worn in gummed rolls, after the Mohave style. Both sexes often used a feather rope or boa to tie the hair at the neck or on top of the head; also at times a head band (tcīta'ka, P; hele'la, N) of plucked beaver skin, about three fingers wide and ornamented with beads.

The hair was cut, with an obsidian knife, only as a sign of mourning for some near relative. It was hidden away or buried with the corpse, to prevent its falling into the hands of some malicious shaman, who might cause illness or even death by placing certain medicines upon it and performing special ceremonies over it.

The hair was brushed with the soaproot fiber brush, plate XXXVI, called caka'nī (N) and sakani (C). This was the brush used in connection with grinding meal; sometimes the identical brush might serve both purposes.

The seeds of a plant called yatcatca (C) were put in the hair when one was without lice, as they produced the same feeling as lice. They were picked out in the same way. Feathers were worn frequently in the hair. Flowers, too, were worn, particularly as wreaths. The showy flowers of the Tiger Lily, *Lilium pardalinum* (palauda, N; palauta, C), the bulb of which was said to be poisonous, were used for wreaths, as were also the flowers (kayu, C) of the Common Monkey Flower, *Mimulus guttatus* (puksa, C). The flowers of another *Mimulus* (hosina, C) were twisted in the hair by children. The yellow flowers of a plant called yonotolu (C) were also used for wreaths. Men used a comb (ta.isa, C), made of about ten small sticks of mountain mahogany, tied side by side with milkweed fiber strings.

The hair net (wayaka, C), (plate LXII, figs. 3 and 4) was worn for dancing, gambling, and when wishing to be dressed up about the house. It was not worn when hunting. Sometimes young women wore the hair net, when dressed for dancing, but it was not worn by old women. The chief might wear daily a hair net, sometimes a beaded one. Other men usually did not wear a hair net daily, as this was regarded as the chief's privilege. A hair net of cotton string, from West Point, Calaveras county, is forty-six inches long. It is number 64514 of the Peabody Museum of American Archaeology and Ethnology, Harvard University.

The hair was washed and lathered with soaproot (palawi, C) every few days, as it was believed to make it grow luxuriantly. Each person washed his own hair, at the creek in warm weather, at home in cold weather.

The men had naturally a considerable growth of hair on the face. Some allowed it to grow and wore a beard of fair size, called mū′sūlī (P) and mūsūpe′lū (N).[85] Others plucked the beard. The body hair was never plucked. The leaves of the white fir were placed in the axillaries by both men and women as deodorizers, when perspiring excessively.

TATTOOING

Tattooing (sina, C) was practiced by both sexes. It was purely decorative and the usual design extended from the edge of the lower lip to the umbilicus. Below the Adam's apple the design (hūsū′ssa, P, N) was always a straight line an inch or less in width. The design above the Adam's apple was either a straight line or one branching upward into three lines. It was called ye′tkū (P, N), and sūka′nu (C). In addition, designs were placed on the shoulders, arms, hands, chest, belly, and thighs. Tattooing was usually done at an early age,

---

[85]Gifford, 1917, pl. 6.

most often between twelve and fifteen, but it was also employed medicinally, the skin directly over a severe pain being tattooed.

The black ashes of the aromatic root of a plant called kū'ya (P, N), probably angelica, supplied the pigment. The scarifier was a sharp point of obsidian or flint, set in the end of a stick about the size of a lead pencil. With this instrument the area to be tattooed was thoroughly pricked until the blood flowed freely. The black ashes were then mixed with the blood and rubbed into the tiny wounds.

One Central Miwok woman, observed in 1913, had lines tattooed on her neck, reputed to have cured consumption. There was a horizontal line on each side of the neck, extending from the side toward the trachea, and two parallel lines down the neck from the anterior ends of these. Another Central Miwok woman, seventy-eight years old, had the following marks: (1) A line, two inches long, across the under side of the left arm, put on with poison oak juice and fine charcoal. (2) Dots on the chin. (3) Her nasal septum and ears were pierced for ornaments. A third woman had the following marks on her left hand and arm. On the back of her hand was a cross, the two lines of which were each one and a half inches long. Across the back of her wrist were a line and three or four dots.

PIGMENTS

Black paint, kula (P, N), for poles and human bodies, was made of charcoal. White paint, ō'ūōū (P, N) was made of chalk (walañasu, C), which in Central Miwok territory was obtainable from the bottom of springs at Springfield.

Red paint, a'wa (P, N) and moke (C), was a mineral pigment, brought by the Eastern Mono to trade for arrows, baskets, and other things. A lump of red pigment as big as one's fist could be purchased with a common basket a few inches high and a few inches in diameter. There is said to be a whole mountain of this red mineral east of the Sierra Nevada, in Eastern Mono territory; also a mountain (Yololamü) containing it, in Central Miwok territory, between lake Eleanor and Cherry river. From this place the Miwok obtained red paint for dancers, as well as getting it by trade from the Mono.

All three pigments were pulverized in water. Sometimes the red pigment was first rubbed to a powder on a stone. To the face the pigment was applied with a flexible stick. The hand was used as the brush in painting large poles. The Miwok rarely used paints for personal ornamentation, as did their Mono neighbors to the east. At ceremonies black, red, and white paints were used. Black was sometimes applied with the end of a charred stick, such as that shown in plate LXIII, fig. 3.

Aside from ceremonial uses there appears to have been but slight application of paint to the face and body. The sleepy catchfly, *Silene antirrhina,* was used to paint the faces of young girls. This plant has a brown, sticky substance on portions of its stems. This was used for the linear design, often horizontal. On the face, the brown adhesive turns black. It was used purely as a cosmetic and had no connection with first menstruation observances.

EAR AND NOSE PIERCING

Both ears and the nasal septum were pierced in childhood. The perforation was called tü'ka (P, N). The piercing was done with an elder needle (tasina, C) while the child slept, or, if awake, the ears were pinched until numb, before the thrust was made. Usually the piercing was done in summer. The age of the children varied from infancy to almost puberty. A girl was operated on always before the first menstruation. The piercing was done by the mother or grandmother. When first pierced and still sore, the perforations were kept open with a stem of supputkululu (C) grass, which was likened to silver in not hurting the pierced flesh. After healing, the apertures were progressively enlarged by thrusting additional stems of grass into the openings. The holes in boys' ears were made largest, as men wore ornaments of larger diameter than women. Young girls and boys wore flowers of the grass *Briza minor* (seppute, C) in their ears, with the flower head forward, the stem passing through the hole.

An earring, consisting of a small string of beads and shells, was called tcū'kkelu (C). An ear plug (lü'sa, P, N; sū'laiu, somayu C) was made by charring the surface of a piece of young pine from four to seven inches in length. When this blackened surface was rubbed down properly it became very shiny. The ends were then ornamented with beads and shells, and sometimes with the scarlet feathers of the California woodpecker. Both sexes wore earrings and earplugs; but the former were used chiefly by the women, the latter by the men. Except among the wealthy and important people these adornments were used only on ceremonial occasions. The same applies to the nose sticks (pīlē′ki, P, N; tu′la, C), some of which were made of white, polished bone, about the diameter of a lead pencil, and from four to nine inches in length; not etched or otherwise ornamented, but highly polished and slightly pointed at the ends. Shell nose sticks (pileki, N; pileku, C) were also worn.

Bird bone tubes five inches long were worn as ear plugs by men. They were made of sandhill crane, or other large bird, bones. Usually white feathers (posesa, C) projected from the ends. Such tubes worn by malevolent shamans (tuyuku, C) were believed to serve as repositories for their "poison."

HEAD DEFORMATION

Heads were habitually deformed, being flattened in the back by the hard cradle; and the forehead pressed and rubbed from center to sides with the mother's hands, to make a short and flat head. This pressing was done each morning and whenever the mother was holding the baby. The process of forehead flattening was called petubak (C). Moreover, the nose was pressed to flatten it, and the eyebrows were rubbed apart.

MOURNING NECKLACE[86]

Plate LXIII, fig. 2, shows a mourning necklace consisting of string with seven tiny cloth bags containing medicine roots. The use of cloth is, of course, a modern innovation. The string was tied about its owner's neck at the funeral of her husband by her husband's sister. Custom required that it remain there until it wore off or until the widow attended a mourning ceremony. During this period she was prohibited from marriage and from associating much with men. Indeed, for a few months after her husband's death she remained entirely secluded with a single woman attendant. The regulations were more rigorously observed by women of rank.

DANCE ORNAMENTS

The most important articles of dance costume were the feather plume, the flicker feather head band, the magpie feather crown, and the feather skirt. With these were used certain auxiliary items, such

---

[86]See *wormwood*, under "Medicines."

as paints, ear plugs, nose sticks, bead necklaces, and belts, clouts and skirts. Also there were objects carried by the dancers, such as the feather ropes borne by women, and the beads, arrows, feather sticks, and imitation bear claws, carried by the men. The music consisted of songs accompanied by the foot drum, the split stick clapper rattle, and the bone whistle.

The feather plume (ma'kkī, P, N, C) consisted of feathers tied upon a stick about a foot long and about the diameter of a lead pencil (plate LXXII, figs. 1-4, and Kroeber, 1925, fig. 21d, e). These feathers might be attached to the end of the stick only, or they might be arranged so as to completely cover it. In the former case the remainder of the stick was wound and covered with eagle down. The feathers were lashed on with a tight winding of string. The rods projecting upward from the center of the feather bunches are tightly wound with red thread (not Miwok). These slender rods are inserted in the wooden handle. Small triangular or rectangular abalone bangles and glass beads (not Miwok) are attached to the projecting iron wire rods (not Miwok) of one example, in which the wrappings are of American red cloth. Little squares of flicker quills are attached to the feather plumes, suspended by string from the middle of one edge. Variation in the little squares of flicker quills was attained by inserting whitish or blackish quills at intervals among the pink ones. The elaborate feather plumes were employed in dances only, while the ordinary ones were worn daily by chiefs and other men of importance. They were usually worn in pairs, being so placed in the hair as to project forward at an angle from the top of the head. Turkey feathers (not Miwok) are employed in part in the feather head ornaments. In one example even guinea fowl feathers are present. Plate LXXII, fig. 5, depicts one feather ornament (sonolu, C) carried in the hand. Apparently rather large stiff tail feathers were used. The outer half of the quill of each has been cut or torn off, possibly to make the feathers more flexible.

The flicker feather head band, plate LXXIII, (tama'kkilī, P, N; tamikila, C) was made of the salmon pink shafts of the primaries of the flicker, laid side by side and sewed through to form an elongated mat (Kroeber, 1925, pl. 58). These were bordered by the dark brown feathers: in one specimen tail feathers; in the other, wing feathers. It was worn in two ways: (1) attached by its middle so as to form a horizontal band across the forehead, with the two ends floating; (2) fas-

tened on top of the head by one end, so as to pass over the crown of
the head and hang down the back.

The feather crown (tī'ūka, P, N) was made entirely of the tail
feathers of the magpie. It comprised two wooden rings of equal diam-
eters with the feathers attached to form an erect cylinder. The lower
of these two rings fitted over the head, while the other was fastened
some distance up on the inside of the cylinder and thus held the feathers
erect. The quills of the feathers were painted red. This headdress
was held in place by a string passing under the chin. It was used in the
lo'le (a women's dance) and the hī'we (a men's dance).

The feather cloak or skirt (sīhlī'wa, P, N; metikila, C) was made
by attaching wing and tail feathers to a net (plates LXIV and LXV).
The feathers of the crow, turkey vulture, magpie, and Western Red-tail
Hawk were employed, but never eagle feathers, because they gave bad
luck. Plate LXIV, fig. 2,[87] has Great Horned Owl and hawk feathers.
The dark feathers on its lower part are perhaps magpie and vulture.
Figure 1 is apparently all magpie feathers. In both of these specimens
the mesh is about forty-five millimeters square. Another specimen
(1-9977) has turkey feathers on a netting of white cotton string, with
meshes about fifteen millimeters square. Figure 1 has a double, bone
whistle and a little mat of flicker quills attached. The two whistles
are of unequal lengths and give different tones. The short one
(50 mm.) is of the humerus of the Sierra Grouse *(Dendragapus
obscurus)*. The long one (70 mm.) is of the tibia of a jackrabbit
(Lepus californicus). The pair of whistles attached to figure 2 are of
jackrabbit tibias. The feather cloak was tied about the arm pits, hanging down the back to about the knees, and was worn for nearly every
dance. When worn by the character called motcilo (C) in the kuksuyu
performance, it was called tcakala (C).

The Peabody Museum of American Archaeology and Ethnology, at
Harvard University, possesses a set of dance regalia (64521) from
the Northern Miwok of West Point, Calaveras county. Included in this
is a dance stick of solid wood (not elder), probably such as is used
by a master of ceremonies. It is forty-eight inches long, with three
encircling bunches of feathers in the upper twenty-two inches. The
upper and lower bunches of feathers are black and appear to be turkey
vulture feathers. The lower encircling bunch has a few flicker feathers

---

[87]Kroeber, 1925, pl. 80.

on its exterior. The middle bunch is of hawk feathers. All feathers are split along the middle. There is a painted, encircling, black band, one inch wide, between each two bunches of feathers. At the bottom there is a similar band one and one-quarter inches wide. At the base of the lowest bunch of feathers there is an encircling band of modern red and yellow glass beads. Below the base of the upper bunch of feathers hangs a little square composed of the salmon-pink flicker quills. There are also two such flicker quills inserted base first in a hole drilled through the stick just below the upper bunch of feathers.

The feather rope (hū'na, P, N) carried by the women in certain dances was made of goose feathers or down twisted into a rope about six feet in length. Comparable with this feather rope for the women were the strings of beads, feather sticks, and arrows carried by the men, these varying according to the dance.

Down was attached to the faces of dancers by first sprinkling them with water. It was stored in small pouches, made by everting the skin of the Western Red-tail Hawk's leg (plate LXIII, fig. 5).

Earplugs by men and nasal septum ornaments by women were worn in the Central Miwok hekeke (valley quail) dance. For dances men used a plain hair net, but for non-ceremonial wear one with abalone bangles.

BASKETRY

Miwok basketry employs several varieties of the two general techniques of twining and coiling. The terms recorded for basketry in general are pūlū'tcī (P); pūla'ka (N); pūla'kka, pūlī'ssa, and allū'mma (C, S). The term mū'ta (C) is applied to white pliable elements used in both coiled and twined basketry, obtained from the young shoots of maple, hazel, willow, pine, oak, redbud, deer brush, and squaw bush.

Miwok basketry in general is characterized by the very extensive use of willow, *Salix* (tcō'pa, P, N; so'so, N; lī'ma, C), for the warp and woof of twined baskets, and for the foundation of coiled baskets. For the wrapping of the latter, redbud, *Cercis occidentalis* (lüli, N; тарáтарu, C; tapátapa, S) is the preferred material. Southern and Central Miwok basketry shows the influence of the adjacent Yokuts and Shoshonean cultures. This is most apparent in the use of the multiple-grass foundation and the number of typically Shoshonean forms and designs.   Plains and Northern basketry is very similar to north-central Californian basketry.

TWINED BASKETRY

The best Miwok twined basketry (te'we, *tewu*'asī, N; тɛwua', C) is relatively coarse compared with the best work of the Washo[88] and Mono.   The burden baskets are nearly all without ornamental patterns, thus contrasting with certain of the Maidu, Washo, and Mono burden baskets.   To utilize even their most closely woven burden baskets for seed gathering, the Miwok had first to fill the interstices with a coating of soaproot (palawi, C) juice, so that the seeds would not work through. The Washo, Maidu, and Mono wove certain of their burden baskets so finely that no coating was required to prevent leakage of seeds.   The Miwok formerly had no finely woven and patterned winnowers like those of the Washo[89] and Mono.

Twined baskets were woven with the fingers alone, except for occasionally tightening a round with a bone awl, or sewing on a reinforcing hoop at the rim with the same instrument.   All Miwok twined baskets, other than cradles, in the University's collection, have reinforcing willow hoops sewed to their rims.   There are no delicate and beautiful twined baskets.

Plates LI–LV show some of the forms of twined baskets.   The Miwok names for the various types are as follows:

Burden basket: tcū'nik, tû'inī (P); tcī'kele, tū'yūma (N); tcī'kele, tcikali, mutak (C); tcī'kele (S).   Plate LIV.

Seed beater: ku'kūsī (N), kūkū'si (C), tca'mai (S).   Plates LI, fig. 3; LII, fig. 3; LIII, fig. 7.

Triangular winnower: he'*talu*, tu'ma (N), tcamayu (C).   This is the closely woven Mono-Washo type.[90]   The names applied are those already in use for the Miwok coiled, circular, winnowing plaque, and openwork, twined, plate-form sifter.

Plate-form, openwork sifter: ū'lit (P); *u*lī'ta, tu'ma (N); he'tal*u* (C); he'tal (S).

Hemispherical, openwork sifter: o'woy*u*, tca'ma (C).   Plate LII, figs. 4-6.

[88]Barrett, 1917, pls. 11 and 13.
[89]Barrett, 1917, pl. 11.
[90]See Barrett, 1917, pl. 11.

Triangular, openwork sifter: tī'lik (P); tca'ma, tca'mai, dja'ma (N); tca'ma, tca'mai̯ (C); tca'mai, tce'kla (S). Plates LII, figs. 1 and 2, and LIII, figs. 4-6 and 8.

Globose storage basket, either closely woven or openwork: tu'pulū, hupulu (C); tū"pūla, hū'pūlū (S).

Fish basket: kesa'pu̯ (C).

Cradle, northern type: tco'ta (P), hī'kī (N). Kroeber, 1925, plate 39f.

Cradle, southern type: woa'na (P, N), hi'kī (C), hī'ki̯ (S). Kroeber, 1925, plate 39a, c-e.

Cradle hood: tcû'kno, tco'kime (C); tcō'kīme (S). Kroeber, 1925, plate 39a.

Rackets for women's ball game: ama"ta (P); tcama'tī (N); a'mta, ammutna (C). Plate LV, figs. 1 and 2.

In the following discussion of materials employed in making twined baskets, the Miwok baskets in the Field Museum of Natural History are included. Identification of basket materials in that collection was by Dr. J. W. Hudson, in the University's collection by Miss Ruth Earl Merrill. The statistics refer to the combined collections.

As warp for twined baskets the identified materials used, in order of abundance, were the stems of *Salix* in 34 examples, *Corylus rostrata californica* in 6, *Cercis occidentalis* in 3, *Rhus trilobata* in 3, *Acer macrophyllum* (pī'pum, N; pī'punû, sa'iyi, C) in 2, and *Ceanothus integerrimus* in 1.

Willow *(Salix)* was also the most abundant weft material. Twenty-three baskets employed *Salix* stems and bark, 11 *Acer macrophyllum* sapwood, 5 *Cercis occidentalis* sapwood, 3 *Rhus trilobata* (ta'ma, C), 3 *Acer macrophyllum* bark, 1 *Corylus rostrata californica* stems, and 1 *Pinus ponderosa* root. *Acer macrophyllum* bark served as binding for a rim hoop in one basketry tray.

Two plain-twined techniques were used. In one a single rod was included in each twining of the pliable elements, in the other two rods. The former is well illustrated in the cradles in Kroeber, 1925, plate 39, the latter in plates LII, fig. 2, and LIV, fig. 2. The latter technique was the commoner. Often the courses of twining elements were run alternately to right and left (plates LII, fig. 4, and LIII, fig. 4). The beginning of a twined basket was called solu (C).

The diagonal-twined technique was occasionally used (plate LIII, fig. 2). The figured example has a handle which is presumably a modern innovation. A second handled example (1–10295) has a design in redbud bark. The weft elements in the courses of design are split redbud stems with the bark on one side. By turning these, either the red bark or the whitish wood is exposed to make the pattern, which is alternating parallelograms of red and white. Where a red figure shows on the exterior, a white one shows on the interior, and vice versa. Both of these diagonal-twined baskets are oval in shape. The beginning of each was made by laying the transverse warp elements side by side and binding a bundle of about six longitudinal warp elements at right angles across them. This bundle is on the inside of the completed basket. The rods in the bundle spread fan fashion from each end of the bundle to form the two ends of the basket. One of the baskets has a single decorative round of three-strand twining, two inches below the rim. Three-strand twining is rare among the Miwok and occurs either as a decorative or a strengthening device, as in burden baskets.

The triangular winnowers used in recent years, were either imported from the Mono and Washo, or made in imitation of their utensils. The ancient Miwok form was a coiled circular plaque (plates XLIX, figs. 2-5, and L, fig. 1). For the triangular winnower young shoots of *Ceanothus cuneatus* (paiwa, C) frequently formed the warp. Older shoots were used for the rim.

The burden basket (plate LIV) was more or less openly twined. Its pointed bottom was usually reinforced with extra weaving elements or with rawhide (plate LIV, fig. 2), since this was the part subjected to the greatest wear. When the bottom was worn through it was repaired with raw deer or other skin. This basket was carried by means of a buckskin or woven burden band, never by means of a woven net. The openness of the weave made this basket unsuitable for carrying fine materials, such as grass seeds. This was overcome by a coating of mucilaginous soaproot juice. The soaproot was baked in hot ashes, dipped in water, and rubbed on the basket. Plate LIV, fig. 3, shows a basket freshly treated in this manner. Such a coated basket was called waka (C). The edge of the burden basket was made rigid by means of a hoop, often of *Ceanothus cuneatus,* and in some a hoop was placed midway down the inside of the basket. The edge of the basket, before the hoop was sewed on, was formed of the projecting warp rods, which were bent over and lashed tightly. In some examples only every fourth or fifth warp rod is bent over, the others being cut off (plate LIV, fig. 2).

Most of the burden baskets were begun by crossing a number of the warp rods and bending them to form the sides of the cone. In two examples (1–10148, 1–10095), the apex of the basket was reinforced with three-strand twining. In three examples a different procedure was adopted, the ends of the warp rods being simply lashed to form a bundle. On two of these a leather cap is sewed over the ends, making a more pointed bottom (plate LIV, fig. 2). Owing to the conical form of burden baskets the number of warp rods was increased as the work proceeded. Consequently the new ones reached only part way down the side of the basket toward the pointed bottom.

Of fourteen burden baskets examined by Miss Merrill, twelve were made in whole or in part of willow. Of these twelve, seven have both willow warp and woof, two have willow warp and maple bark woof, three have hazel warp and willow woof. Figure 4 of plate LIV, with willow warp, from West Point (N), has the first few courses of woof of grapevine, at the point of the basket, while the remainder is of split willow stems. The rim hoop is also bound on with grapevine. In figure 1 of plate LIV the courses of twining for about two inches below the rim are close together. For two inches below this a crude ornamental band has been formed by using redbud bark as one of the two strands of woof.

A miniature burden basket (1–10091) from Murphys, in Central Miwok territory, is the only Miwok basket which employs hazel for both warp and woof. Another burden basket (1–10163) is made entirely of peeled redbud and has an ornamental band of redbud bark about two inches below the rim. The warp is of peeled redbud stems, the woof of redbud sapwood.

With the coated burden basket was used the handled seed beater. One (plate LIII, fig. 7) has the handle at right angles to the scoop of the basket. The opposite extreme in the position of the handle is shown in plate LII, fig. 3. Here the handle is in nearly the same plane as the scoop. Specimen 70029, Field Museum, is a deep, nearly circular Central Miwok seed beater with a ring finish at the end of the handle, made by bending over and wrapping the warp elements, as around the edge of a twined basket. It was used as a scoop as well as a flail. In the Peabody Museum of Archaeology and Ethnology there is a Miwok seed beater of the Cahuilla type. It consists of a number of folded twigs, bundled at one end to form a handle and expanded fanlike at the folded or bent middles of the twigs. A circular withe, and two cross rods lashed together on either side across the diameter of the circle, serve to hold the twigs rigidly in position. Plate LI, fig. 3, shows this specimen.

Variation in color of the Miwok seed beater was attained in some cases by using alternate groups of peeled and unpeeled willow sticks for the warp elements. Young sprouts of deer brush, *Ceanothus integerrimus* (ūsū'nni, C, S) were also used. There was variation in the placing of the hoop forming the edge of the flatter seed beaters, for in some cases it passes under the base of the handle (plate LII, fig. 3), and in other cases over. Seed beaters were sometimes used to leach manzanita cider (e.g., 1-10186).

When seeds were obtained they were usually sifted and winnowed before being stored. The sifting was done with the coarsely twined basket of more or less triangular form (plates LII, figs. 1, 2, 4-6, and LIII, figs. 6, 8). These also served for cleaning shelled acorn meats, to rid them of the brown coating, sometimes for leaching small quantities of acorn meal, for leaching manzanita cider, and for draining boiled clover.

Small openwork baskets were hung up as receptacles for awls, other small implements, and trinkets (e.g., 1-10096 and plate LIII, figs. 1, 3).

The Central and Southern Miwok, at least, used large, globose, twined, storage baskets called hupulu for the storing of greens, dried fish, and other dried foods. Some were so large that the maker got inside the partly finished basket to work on it. A twined storage basket of the hū'pūlū (S) type is in the Field Museum collection (70040), from the Chowchilla river in Southern Miwok territory. It is about 10 inches high and 19 in diameter, and both warp and woof are of redbud.

CRADLES

One of the most striking differences in the basketry of the Northern and Southern Miwok is in the cradles. In the north the cradle was not a basket, but was made of two hooked oaken sticks with wooden slats bound across, as shown in plate LXXIV, fig. 3. The two curved ends were placed at the top and served as the support of the face covering of the infant (Kroeber, 1925, pl. 39*f*). In the south a twined cradle was used, as shown in plate LXXIV, fig. 4.

The Field Museum of Natural History has two examples of the northern type of cradle (70237, Chicken Ranch, Tuolumne county; 70238, Bald Rock, Tuolumne county). Both have parallel bent sticks of oak; 70237 has cross pieces of elder and 70238, of chaparral. The width of 70237 at the bottom is 265 mm. Both have modern cloth carrying straps. In 70237 there are six extra cross sticks bound on the inside of the cradle where it begins to curve upward. These may have served as a sort of head-rest. In 70237, the cross sticks are lashed on with string; in 70238, with chaparral. The lashing in 70238 forms a figure **8** around the terminal part of each cross stick.

Variants of the woven cradle with willow warp are shown in plate LXXIV, fig. 2, and plate LXXV, figs. 1 and 2. Also in Kroeber, 1925, plate 39*a*, and *c-e*. These range from the small and very simple woven "board" (plate LXXIV, fig. 2) without any reinforcement, to the cradle reinforced with cross bars at the back (plate LXXIV, fig. 4), or with similar bars on the front (plate LXXV, fig. 2). Plate LXXV, fig. 1, has a complete hoop to reinforce it. In plate LXXIV, fig. 2, is shown a peculiar hemispherical, hoop-like frame for a complete cover for the face of the sleeping baby. All these hoods served primarily to keep the covering from touching the face. The hood in plate LXXIV, fig. 4, is copied after Mono and Washo models and is made of deer brush. The hood is woven apart from the bed of the cradle and is then attached to it. In this example the lashings are of cotton cloth. The hood is concavo-convex, of plain twining, with the woof courses quite far apart. A band of four to seven rods, held together by twining on its two terminal portions, is attached to the under side of the hood, in this example, with worsted. In this specimen the worsted forms a diamond pattern both on the upper and under sides of the hood. Zigzag lines or diamonds indicated a girl baby; the same plus vertical lines on each side indicated a boy baby. The hoods of true Miwok cradles gave no indication of the sex of the baby. Plate LXXIV, fig. 1, Central Miwok, the white strip of cloth forms a zigzag design on both sides.

Plate LXXIV, fig. 2, shows the type of cradle in which the Northern

Miwok baby was kept until a month old. Thereafter the type shown in plate LXXIV, fig. 3, was employed.

At the present time cradles are provided with more or less soft pads like that in the cradle just mentioned. In aboriginal times, however, swaddling clothes (pa'ka, P, N) were made of a soft marsh grass procured in the lowlands. This was beaten between stones and shredded with a bone awl to make it as fine and soft as possible. The child was carefully wrapped and was bound into the cradle by means of a cord laced back and forth through loops on either edge of the "board." The cradle was ordinarily used until the child was about two years old. Two cradles shown in plate LXXV, figs. 3 and 4, are types from adjacent tribes and are here shown for comparison.

COILED BASKETS

The foundation rods (tcu'lüme, N; sa'pu, C) of coiled baskets were gathered when the plants were in their prime, and were stored in bundles or coils for use during the remainder of the year. For certain coiled baskets, rods ten feet long were used. Some baskets were coiled clockwise, others contra-clockwise.

In the discussion of materials the Field Museum specimens are combined with the University's. The identification of plant materials in the former collection was by Dr. J. W. Hudson, in the latter by Miss Ruth Earl Merrill.

For foundation materials 59 coiled baskets had *Salix,* 33 *Epicampes rigens californica,* 20 *Rhus trilobata,* 7 *Prunus demissa,* 4 *Corylus rostrata californica,* 4 *Avena,* 3 *Cornus glabra,* 1 *Cercis occidentalis,* 1 *Pinus ponderosa* root. The last also had the same material for wrapping. Informants mentioned, as also used for foundation, *Lonicera hispidula* (pipenu, C) stems and a grass (cū'lupü, lī'ma, N; sū'lpanû, C; hū'lūp, S). Perhaps this grass is *Epicampes rigens.*

The Northern Miwok use *Epicampes* grass less frequently for foundations than do the Central and Southern Miwok. It occurs as foundation in 4 Northern, 17 Central, and 10 Southern baskets. The adjacent Maidu on the north do not employ the plant for basketry even though it grows in their territory.[91] The Washo, however, use it. Hazel is

---

[91]Merrill, map 6.

another material used scantily by the Miwok, but not at all by the Maidu.[92]

For wrapping or sewing materials the following were noted: *Cercis occidentalis* sapwood in 73 baskets, *Carex barbarae* (sū'lī, P, N, C; pa'iwa, S) root in 21, *Rhus trilobata* in 13, *Acer macrophyllum* (sayi, C) sapwood in 8, *Pinus ponderosa* rootlet in 4, *Carex robusta* in 3, and *Cyperus virens* in 1.

The Miwok of the Upper Sonoran life zone used the slender twigs of the digger pine as white sewing material. The twigs were gathered in the spring when the bark slips off easily. They were hacked off with a sharp stone flake (tepelila, C), sometimes even of granite, not a knife. The inner woody portion was split into four sections. The splitting was begun at the outer or small end of the twig, the outer end of the twig being bitten in half longitudinally. Then one-half of the split end was held between the teeth, while the fingers carefully guided the splitting for the full length. The unsplit portion was held rather tightly between the right thumb and forefinger. With the left hand the loose half was pulled downward. Simultaneously the right hand was slid downward, so that the splitting took place just above the right thumb and forefinger which guided the course of the splitting, while the left hand furnished the motive power. Thereafter the two halves were similarly split into quarters. The pith was removed from each quarter by biting it free at the small end first. The woody portion was then held in the teeth and the separation of pith and wood continued for the length of the quarter with the fingers. Sugar pine twigs were too brittle for use; no part of the sugar pine was used for basketry.

Slough grass *(Carex barbarae)* root yielded a fine white material, usually found in the finer baskets, and used especially by the lowlanders, in whose territory this plant abounded. The mountaineers often used other and coarser white elements because of the scarcity of the slough grass in their country. The roots of the slough grass are brown externally and about three-sixteenths of an inch in diameter. The roots were split to obtain the white material within. The sapwood of the maple *(Acer macrophyllum)* was obtained only in spring when the bark slips off readily. The shoots were too tough to be broken off by hand and were cut off with a sharp fragment of stone, unworked. They were then scraped with a flake of gray stone called kolubu (C).

---

[92]Merrill, map 3.

The redbud bark for patterns was obtained to best advantage after the sap had begun to run. The outer bark yielded a red, decorative material, which was used particularly in the mountains.

Three brown or black elements were employed. (1) Fern (*Pellaea mucronata*), kepekü (C), roots, sometimes twenty feet long, were dug for the brown covering which was stripped off. The roots were usually dug from a vertical bank where removal was easy. (2) Bracken (*Pteris aquilina*), sī′na (P, N, C), *ta′*tama (P, N), roots were most used for brown and black patterns. (3) The third plant, the root of which yielded a brown material (mu′lla, C, S), was not identified. These materials were brownish when taken from the plants. They were dyed black by placing them in warm ashes, dyeing with green manzanita charcoal pulverized in warm water, boiling in certain mud, or in water with fresh black oak bark. In the Field Museum and in the University's museum there are forty-six coiled baskets with designs in redbud and seventy with designs in bracken. Of the latter in the University's collection five had the material mud-dyed and one manzanita charcoal dyed.

Feathers were said to have been formerly employed for fine basketry decoration. Red feathers were obtained from the California Woodpecker (*Melanerpes formicivorus*), paltī′na (P), pala′tata (N, C, S); the Pileated Woodpecker (*Hylotomus pileatus*), pa′kpaku (C); and the Red-winged Blackbird (*Agelaius phoeniceus*), tcīkūppa′tī (P). The Mallard (*Anas platyrhynchos*), sīnahī′ka (P), hī′kasü (N), yielded green feathers, the Meadowlark (*Sturnella neglecta*), yū′kū′lī (P), pī″na (N), yellow feathers; and the Brewer's Blackbird (*Euphagus cyanocephalus*) black feathers. The plumes from the crests of the Valley Quail (*Lophortyx californica*) and the Mountain Quail (*Oreortyx picta*) were also used.

These various materials were manipulated and woven with the hands. The only tool was the bone awl, which was used to pierce the finished part of the basket, to make an opening through which to pass the sewing material. A series of these awls is shown in plate XXXIX.

The starting knot (sayu, C) in many coiled baskets is a small, tightly bound coil of fine maple or sedge splints, or of the leaf of *Iris hartwegii* (yotowina, C). These must be very fine to permit bending at a very sharp curve. Such a special starting knot is unnecessary in the multiple-grass foundation basket, since the grass, when wet, is very pliable.

The border of a coiled basket was often left with only the finish of the last round of sewing (plate XLVIII, fig. 6). A more careful finish was plain whipping over or sewing of the edge (plate XL). An ornamental edge was furnished by a similar, but diagonal whipping (plate XLIX, fig. 4, and plate L, fig. 2); and a more ornamental finish was formed by two opposing diagonal sewings which formed a herring-bone design. All these border finishes were called tū'llī and mumbilo (C).

TECHNIQUES

Two kinds of coiling, the single-rod foundation (plate XLVII) and the three-rod foundation (plate XL) prevailed throughout the entire Sierra Miwok region. The two-rod foundation was occasionally used. The multiple-grass foundation (plate XLI) was much used by the Central and Southern Miwok.

The single-rod foundation technique was made in the usual way, but frequently in thrusting the awl point through the basket a rod was pierced and split so that at first sight the basket may appear to be of multiple-welt foundation. So far, however, no true multiple-welt basket has been found among the Miwok.

The two-rod foundation was employed, at least in the Central and Southern areas. Informants stated that it was not used in the Northern and Plains areas. In this technique two rods of unequal diameter were placed side by side in each coil, the larger rod being on the inside. Owing to this inequality in the rods the outward appearance of a basket of this technique is similar to that of a three-rod foundation basket. As in the single-rod foundation, the piercing of the rods by the awl produced what in cross-section might appear as a multiple-welt or a rod-and-multiple-welt foundation.

The three-rod foundation technique was much used. Again we find the careless splitting of the rods. In an unusual form of this technique there is no superimposition of the rods, but a large central rod is flanked on either side by a small one, called matcī'nu (C). The sewing element is intentionally passed through the large rod at each stitch.

The multiple-grass foundation consists of a bundle of fine grass stems. The manipulation of the sewing element is quite the same as in the other coiled techniques.

Split stitches occur rarely in Central Miwok coiled baskets. No name was obtainable for this peculiarity. An example is shown in plate LI, fig. 2, which is a specimen (74928) in the Peabody Museum of American Archaeology and Ethnology, Harvard University. In this example the stitches are split only on the exterior of the basket. On the interior they are intact. This example is from Calaveras county. An example of lazy stitch is specimen 71544, Field Museum (Southern Miwok, Chowchilla river). Each coil is wrapped three or four times, then a wrapping passes over the adjacent coil.

The designations for the four techniques of coiled baskets are given below. With the exception of the word sū'ta, they seem to be based on the words for the numerals one, two, and three. Single-rod coil: sū'ta (P), lūtī'ka (N), keñe'ka (C). Two-rod coil: ōtī'ko (N), ōtī'ka (C). Three-rod coil: telóka (P, N), ʈelo'ka (C). Multiple-grass coil: telo'ka (N).

The Miwok names for the various forms of coiled baskets are as follows:

Plate-form winnower: ūlī'ta (N), eselo (C), he'talu (S). Plate XLIX, figs. 1-5.

Parching basket: ke'waiyu (C), to'gūn (S). Plates XLVIII, fig. 2; XLIX, fig. 1.

Cooking basket, Maidu type: toyuno (N). Plate XL.

Cooking basket, truncated-cone form: pula'ka, pu'la (N); pūla'ka, ho'motca, ho'nmūtca, tco'ʈi, o'sa (C); alu'mma, hū'lī (S). Plates XLI; XLV, figs. 5 and 6; XLVII, figs. 5 and 6; and XLVIII, fig. 6.

Small truncated-cone basket: hī'ma, ū'līta (C); alumma (S). Plates XLII; XLIII, figs. 5-10; XLIV; and XLVI, figs. 1-4.

Truncated-cone basket, multiple-grass foundation and string: kotī' (S).

Globose basket, not multiple-grass: hīsu'ma (C).

Globose basket, multiple-grass foundation and string: osa sotono (C), pula'kka (S).

Dipper: pulī'sa (P); pudī'sa (N), pūlī'ssa, sō'tonō, (C); pūla'kka (S). Plates XLIII, figs. 2, 4; XLV, figs. 1-3; XLVII, figs. 1, 2; XLVIII, fig. 1; and L, figs. 3, 4.

Low, cylindrical basket: te'waiyu (C).

Elliptical or canoe-form basket: wī'kili (C). Plates XLIII, fig. 3; XLVII, fig. 4; and XLVIII, fig. 3.

Feathered basket: ko'tī (S).

Plate-form, multiple-grass foundation basket: hetalu, o'sa, o'sa sō'tonō (C). Plate L, fig. 1. The plate-form, multiple-grass basket was made mostly in the Southern Miwok area and slightly in the Central. It is doubtless related to the similar baskets of the Yokuts, especially the gambling tray. Two Field Museum examples (70001, 70221) are designated gambling trays.

In cooking and serving acorn mush, soup, and bread, the Miwok employed the closely-woven, flaring basket (plates XLII; XLIII, figs. 5-10; XLIV; XLV, figs. 5, 6; XLVI; and XLVII, figs. 5, 6). The cooking was done in a large basket by means of hot stones (plate XXXII, figs. 1-4), and the cooling and serving in smaller baskets of similar form (plate XLIII, figs. 5, 6; XLV, fig. 3; and XLVII, fig. 3). A very small basket of similar form was used as a dipper for transferring food, and for drinking water or manzanita cider (plate XLIII, figs. 1-4; XLV, figs. 1, 2; XLVII, fig. 1; and XLVIII, fig. 1). Another use was to dip and pour acorn soup, which was done to thicken it while cooking, especially in "biscuit making." The same basket was also employed as a mold for the "biscuits" when placed in cold water.

For feasts, particularly those given by chiefs upon special occasions, large "gift" baskets (plate XL) were usually used for serving food, and sometimes for cooking it, but were never employed at feasts connected with the dead. The one illustrated is Northern Miwok and shows Maidu relationship in its deep conical form, as well as in its ornamentation. It was first given to a young man as a wedding present, and was later used to serve food. When filled, such a basket was very heavy and was carried into the center of the assembly house by several men, using straps tied about it. The food was then dipped out into smaller baskets by two women and served to the gathering. Such a large basket was always owned by a chief and was never communal property. He might present or trade it to another chief, or he might burn it in honor of some departed relative or friend. Such a basket owned by a chief must, upon his death, be burned. Sometimes such a basket held the water for the ceremonial washing of mourners.

A shallow, broad basket (plate XLIX, fig. 1) was used especially for parching seeds, as was also the plate-form meal sifter or winnower.

The elliptical or canoe-form basket (plate XLVIII, fig. 3; and XLVII, fig. 4), the flaring and straight-sided baskets (plate XLVIII, figs. 1, 2, 4-7; and XLVII, fig. 2), and the globose basket (plate XLV, fig. 4) were used as general storage receptacles and for the serving of some kinds of food.

Field Museum specimen 70023 is a Central Miwok single-rod meal basket, about a foot in diameter and ten inches high. It is flat bottomed and vertical walled, forming a perfect cylinder. 70038 is a five-inch, single-rod, coiled basket, about fifteen inches in diameter. It has a slightly incurved rim and was used as a meal or seed bin. It is Central Miwok.

DESIGNS

The designs decorating baskets are simple and the names show an equal simplicity of ideas. In most cases these names indicate geometric forms or are closely related to geometric ideas. A few modifying terms are used in connection with them. The general name for design or pattern is sü'ka (C, S). Very few twined baskets had designs, while virtually every coiled basket did have.

The simple horizontal line or band, or several parallel lines, is frequent. It is called saᴛe'tü or saᴛe'tü tcü (C), *lying down straight;* or pisi'ssi (S), *long stripes* (text-figures 29 and 30). One Central Miwok informant gave this type of design the name lūtū'tta.

A series of parallel, vertical, or nearly vertical, lines (figure 31) is called tcīpu'tcü (C), *standing erect,* and patīwu'nī (S).

The zigzag, horizontally, diagonally, or vertically placed, is called lō'yaa, lōya'asi, or lō'yaûni (C, S), *zigzag* or *crooked.* It may be a single line or a number of lines side by side (figures 32-34, variants in figures 35-37). To'ᴛoᴛo loyaasī (C) is the term for the diagonally placed zigzag. Central informants named the horizontal zigzag kītcē'ya *(arrowhead)* yolō'lī.

Small rectangles connected by their corners to form figures are referred to by the general term lōwō'ᴛa (C), *overlapping, held together,* and *geese* or *flying geese,* because a row of figures suggests a line of flying geese (figures 38-44). Some combinations of rectangles had special names in addition to lōwō'ᴛa (C). Figure 39 was called otī'kō (C), *double;* figure 40 ma'ilutcü (C) *lying down on one's elbow.* Another informant called it wekelē'ya, *stretched out sidewise or lengthwise.* For figure 43 hutū'ta (S), *a row of figures or objects in single file,* was given by one informant. Figure 45 was called weke'lunī (S), *lengthwise, sidewise,* or *stretched out,* and hutūta lī'let (S), *single file*

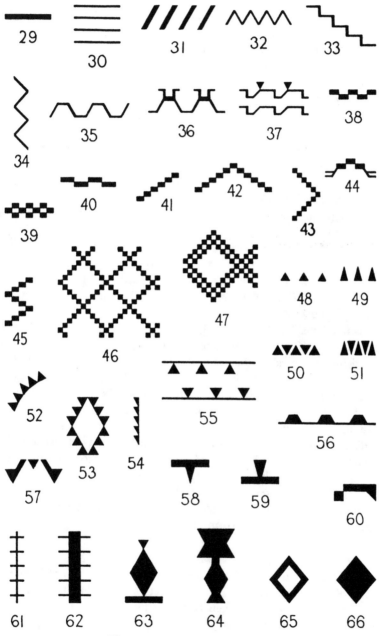

Figs. 29-66.—Basketry designs.

vertical. Crossing lines of rectangles were called lo'yaûni wē'kelēya hutūta (S), *zigzag lengthwise single file.* Similar crossing lines of triangles were called wekelē'ya hutūta (S), *stretched out single file.* Figure 47 was called pīnu'tukkü (C), *stitched* or *sewed up.*

The general term for the designs in figures 48-57 is kītcē'ya (C), *arrowhead.* The straight line in figure 55 was called ma'ilutcü (C), *lying down on one's elbow.* Figure 56 was called hū'mūtcü (C), *moustaches.*

In figure 58 is shown a design which occurs as a single figure or as several such figures superposed. It was called ki'liagû (C), *horn forehead,* and refers to the head of the deer. It was also called mutcilimma kitcē'ya (S), *sharp arrowhead.* Figure 59 was called yuta'ppa (C), *hanging down* or *fastened.* Figure 60 was called tē'wutcü (C), *standing on its legs.*

Figure 61 was called pisa'lla (C), *striped,* and tcamu'a (S), *dead.* The closely related design in figure 62, however, was called hatcī'tcü (C), *standing up* or *resting upon its own base.* Figure 63 also was called hatcī'tcü (C), and tcamū'a (S). Further, this latter term was applied to figure 64.

Diamond-shaped designs, such as the open and the solid ones in figures 65 and 66, respectively, are occasional on Miwok basketry. One Central informant called these o'no, signifying *gold,* apparently derived from Spanish *oro,* and the figures were evidently conceived as nuggets.

The design in figure 67 was called kahō'na tōbe'pa (S). The first part of the term is derived from the Spanish *cajon,* box.

In figures 68-76 are a number of rare designs. Figure 77 was called hosakuna (C), *star.* It was on the bottom of an unfinished coiled basket which began with three-rod coiling and changed to single-rod. Designs 78-84 are additional designs from coiled baskets.

Field Museum basket 70023, from Bald Rock, Tuolumne county, has a design in redbud *(Cercis occidentalis)* in four horizontal courses, said to represent the measuring worm (figure 85).

MATS

The people of the lowlands made mats (he'sī, P) from at least two species of tule, that circular in cross-section, and that triangular in cross-section. Some were seven feet long by three or four feet wide. They were employed principally as sleeping mats, but were spread as

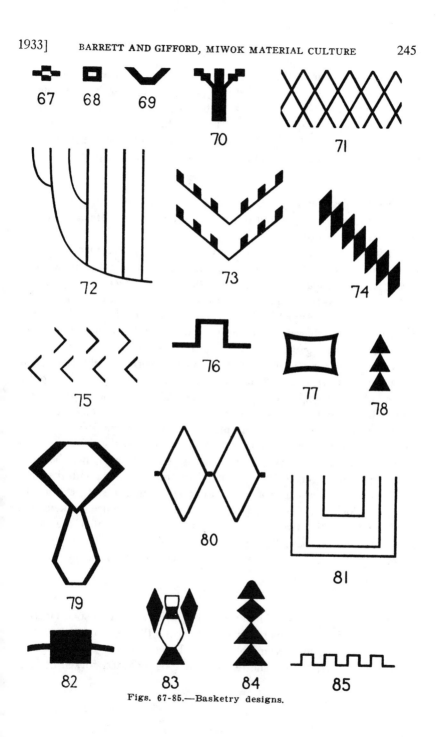

Figs. 67-85.—Basketry designs.

a floor covering during the day and served as a table on which to spread a repast. A mat of a very fine grass (pa'ka, P, N), which grows about springs, was used especially as a "table cloth." This mat was called *u*ta'pan (P) and ūtapû'nu (N). The Northern Miwok made a mat of very fine twigs. The Central Miwok made a mat for the dice game tcaта'tu from a grass (sulupu, C) which grows in wet places.

CORDAGE

The simplest binding was a withe of grapevine or a grass stem. To tie bundles of greens and other plants the Central Miwok used the stem of a sedge *(Carex)* called soma.

String (l*u*ka'bun*u*, N; hūkápa, C; u'mahī, S) was made by both men and women from various bast fibers, especially the milkweeds *Asclepias cordifolia, Asclepias giffordi,* and *A. speciosa* (tī'gūn, P; tī'gunu', N; sū'kkenû, tumuka, C). *Fremontia californica* bast was similarly used, and presumably that of *Apocynum cannabinum.* Milkweed for string was gathered in summer and was dried by placing flat on the ground, or it was gathered in the fall and winter when naturally dry. The fiber used for string was not the outer covering of the stems, but the layer next within, lying between the outer covering and the pithy center. After drying, the stems were combed through a loop of green willow held in the right hand. The combed stems were wound into balls. In this state the fiber was called umazi (C). In spinning, two groups of fibers are tied at one end, then rolled downward on the thigh. As the spinning proceeds, the lower end of the twisted portions is held between the thumb and finger of the left hand. The rolling is done with the right hand, which is spat in from time to time. When a sufficient length has been done, the tied end is held and the string rolled back up the thigh to bring the two elements together and to tighten the twist. Cordage seems to have been generally two-ply, though the Field Museum has Central Miwok examples of three-ply and four-ply cordage as well (70280, 1-3).

NETS

Fish nets were made of milkweed fiber string. A mesh stick (tasena, C, the term for any stick) was used to work the net on, each row of meshes being made over it (plate LVIII, figs. 2-6). The string for the net was carried on a shuttle about a foot long and forked at both ends.

A fish net (70191, Field Museum) from Bald Rock, Tuolumne county, appeared to be made with a flat or reef knot of *Asclepias speciosa* bast. The mesh was eight centimeters square, the cord two millimeters in diameter. The net was three by six feet.

A netting bag, yemalu' (C), was made with milkweed fiber string and used to carry bulbs and corms. The mesh was small and the handle or carrying strap was of netting material. It was carried on the back by suspension from the head or shoulders.

CARRYING STRAPS AND SLINGS

Carrying straps or tump lines are called ela'ia (P), lü'ke (N), and luke (C). The Field Museum of Natural History has a carrying strap (70041) woven of *Asclepias* fiber string, attached to a very pointed, openwork burden basket (70033), from the Central Miwok of Tuolumne county. The strap shown in plate LXXVI is made of string of a different fiber, perhaps *Apocynum,* but is of similar weave. It is said to have been used in carrying a large ceremonial basket and is from the "Southern Mines country, probably Sonora." It is probably Central Miwok or possibly Southern Miwok.

The middle section of the strap is of twined weave and is five feet, three inches long and an inch and a quarter wide. The terminal braided cords of the strap are forty and thirty-two inches long respectively.

We are indebted to Professor Lila M. O'Neale for making a special study of this carrying strap and for the following exact description of the technique employed.

1. Twining warps over weft moving in customary fashion. 22 warps. Regular twining with exception that lower warp crosses to left of 1-11; to right of 12-22, making pattern down center. The weft is a single heavy cord which doubles back and forth across the strap.

2. The ends are of eight-strand braid made by crossing outer right over outer left at center. Repeat.

3. The transition from twining to braiding is made by dividing the warp elements into two bundles and wrapping them in figure eight weave with the single thick weft cord, the end of which is worked into the braid. At one end of the twined portion there are three double courses of figure eight wrapping, at the other end four and five courses. The weft cord was wrapped with a broad straw-like material.

The Field Museum possesses a sling (70263) made of strings of *Asclepias* fibers. This sling has a finger loop, also a buckskin receptacle for the stone to be hurled. It is a Southern Miwok specimen.

SKIN DRESSING

All skin dressing was done by men. The hide was staked out on the ground. Deer hides required no scraping, but bear hides did. A deer hide dried in three or four days. Then it was soaked in a creek for two days. Thereafter it was removed and allowed to drain. Next it was put in a basket with a lubricant solution of pulverized boiled deer brains (lŭ'pet, S), in which it was soaked overnight. The following morning it was removed, wrung out, and pulled, rubbed, and worked to make it pliable and soft. It was thus worked continually until dry, except that the workman stopped for meals. Sometimes the hair was left on; sometimes it was removed by scraping with a sharp tibia. In such a case the hide was put over a post or small stump and the scraper (lutaa, C) drawn down. This natural scraper required no shaping or sharpening, but could be put to immediate use as soon as the flesh was removed from it.

A bear hide was staked out, hair side down, and covered with rotten wood from a hollow tree, to absorb the fat. This was stirred frequently and then the hide was scraped with a sharp-edged piece of wood with long grain. This scraper was called saka (C). The process was repeated for four or five days. There was no dressing as with deer hide, the bear hide being left stiff and hard. Bear skins were used as seats and beds by chiefs only.

Brains were used on any skin which was to be softened, e.g., a fox or wildcat skin. When available, fresh brains were used, but a deer brain cake was made to preserve the brains for this special use. The fresh brains were intermixed with a long water grass, called ki'si (S). This was then made into a discoidal cake, called koso't (S), and dried for preservation. When needed such a cake was boiled for about an hour, and the solution allowed to cool until lukewarm. In specimen 1-10005 cooked deer brains are enclosed in a small bag formed of deer scrotum and tied at the top with a string.

BOATS

The tule balsa (wo'te, C) was used in lagoons and in slack water on the San Joaquin river and on the lower courses of its tributaries. It was made of about twenty cylindrical bundles of tule, called kanō'wa in Central Miwok (cf. Spanish canoa), and was usually about fifteen feet in length by about three or four feet in width. It had a willow pole on each side as a gunwale, and eight willow ribs bound to its outside, for rigidity. It was propelled by one or more paddles, each made from a single piece of wood, and was used for hunting and for transport when moving camp. In the latter case the men swam beside or behind it and pushed it.

In the hills two logs were sometimes tied together to make a raft to cross rivers and large streams.

MUSIC

Music was called kowana (C), a word apparently connected with kowa, musical bow. There were melodies used in every-day life, such as lullabies and love songs. Those connected with medicine and ceremonial practices were of wider range. They comprised songs for good luck in hunting, gambling, and war, also songs used in ceremonial and religious dances.

The musical instruments of the Miwok were few and simple. The foot drum used in the assembly house has been described. Double and single bone whistles (mī′kūya′ke, P; kūya′ke, N) were used in dances (plate LVII, figs. 1-8). An elder whistle was used by Central Miwok shamans in curing the sick, and by dancers among the Southern Miwok (Field Museum 70203).

With the dance whistles were used the split-stick, clapper rattle (taka′tta, P, N) and to a less extent the cocoon rattle (sokō′ssa, C), Handbook, figure 37f. The latter was also used by shamans. It was made of the large gray cocoons of a butterfly. Into the dried cocoons small bits of white stone were introduced. Feathers were often added for ornament. A Northern Miwok example from West Point, Calaveras county, in the Peabody Museum at Harvard University, consisted of three cocoons on a one-foot handle. This was used in the kalea dance. Another cocoon rattle called wasilni (C), differed in being much larger and attached to a four-foot stick. A single cocoon with pebbles, attached to a stick, was called muliya (C). The cocoon rattle shown in Kroeber, 1925, figure 37f has two sticks for the foundation. These are lashed together at the top. Included in the lashing are six large quills upon each of which one of the six cocoons is impaled. Each cocoon contains small seeds which make the rattling or rushing sound when the rattle is shaken. The feathers, perhaps those of the body plumage of a large hawk, are tied in groups of two, three, or four to a string and then the string is wound around the stem of the rattle. The feathers are tied by folding over and lashing the bases of the quills. The string also runs through the loop thus formed by the quills. There appear to be four windings. The string employed is the ordinary commercial cotton string. The diameter of the feather bunch is nine inches. Each feather has the base of its quill cut off. The whole rattle has the appearance of having been smoked. Its double handle of slightly pointed sticks may have been used for insertion in the hair as well as carrying in the hand. Rattles were also made from dew claws of deer.

An elder wood clapper rattle in the Field Museum (70199), from the Southern Miwok of Chowchilla river, Mariposa county, is 535 millimeters long, ten millimeters in diameter, and painted red. Like all elder clappers it has had the pith removed from the split portion. The bisecting of the stick extends from the distal end to within about three inches of the proximal end. These three inches form the handle by which the clapper is held and manipulated. Two other Field Museum examples (70200, 2-3) are from the Central Miwok of Groveland. The first is 855 millimeters long and two centimeters in diameter. The second is 760 millimeters long and about 25 millimeters in diameter.

The flute (lula, C), Kroeber, 1925, plate 43c, was played for courtship and pastime. It had a range of several tones. Informants mentioned six-hole and eight-hole instruments of elder wood. A specimen (70195) in the Field Museum has six holes on one side and one on the opposite side. It is from Groveland in Central Miwok territory. Another (70196) is 672 millimeters long.

The musical bow (kowa, C) was of elder, with a deer-sinew string, twisted on the bare thigh. The Field Museum of Natural History has a Central Miwok example (70206), 1280 mm. in length, from Groveland. In one method of playing the bow was held in the middle between the teeth and the string played with the fingers. In the other method one end of the bow was held in the mouth. The musical bow was usually played by men and for pleasure only. It was not used ceremonially.

The bull-roarer is represented in the collection of the Field Museum of Natural History by two specimens (70201, 70202) from Yosemite valley, collected by Hudson, and reputed to be Southern Miwok. Both are made of pine.

ADHESIVES

Central Miwok informants knew nothing about glue from fish heads. In fact in the mountain region there were few large fish. Soaproot juice and pine pitch seem to have been the only adhesives used. Hot soaproot juice applied to twined burden baskets made their walls impervious to the small seeds placed in them. This same fluid also served to bind the handles of brushes made of soaproot fibers. The use of this mucilaginous fluid on baskets suggests the Mono custom of waterproofing bottle baskets with pine pitch. The use of such utterly different plants for rather similar purposes suggests independent origins. If a single origin is the case, it is remarkable that the plant used by the inventors was not also utilized by the borrowers of the idea.

BEADS

Few or no disk beads were made by the Miwok. They obtained the discoidal clam shell beads chiefly from the people living to the north, while olive shell disks and long tubular beads came from the south. Apparently they themselves regularly made only abalone *(Haliotis)* shell ornaments, and chains of whole olive shells and other univalves.

Beads and shells were employed in necklaces, belts, bandoliers, and shell ropes. No leg or ankle bands were made. The names of these several articles are as follows: necklace, hü'le (P, N), hü'lu (C); belt, tē'pa (P, N), pa'tca (C), lu'ta (C); wrist band, nawu'tta (P, N); bandolier, ta'ime (C); shell rope, kolo'asi (C). All these were extensively used as adornments for dances and ceremonies, and as decorations for corpses.

OLIVE SHELLS

Olive shells *(Olivella biplicata)*, called mutū'gu (P, N), kolo'asi (C), lū'kkū (C), were obtained, at least in part, from Monterey bay. The Costanoan inhabitants of its shores allowed the Miwok to make journeys thither to procure these shells. The Miwok did not appreciate the lustrous grays, browns, and whites of the living shells, and proceeded to destroy the luster and to whiten the shells by gently baking them in the ashes of a fire made of buckeye wood and white oak bark, after which they were sifted from the ashes in an openwork basket.

Care was taken constantly to turn the shells lest they burn to an un-
pleasing brown. Any other wood fire was said to have that effect. A
smaller shell, called ka'ssuᴛu (C), perhaps also an *Olivella,* was similarly treated.

The tip of the spire of the olive shell was ground off, so as to
leave an aperture for stringing (plates LXIII, fig. 4, and plate
LXVI). A string of shells one reach (ana, C) in length was worth one
dollar. The ana was the customary unit of measure for strings of
these shells. Such strings of whole olive shells were used for money
as well as ornament. As ornaments they were draped around the neck
and over the chest, worn as belts, and tied on as headbands.

For olive shell ropes (plate LXVI) the shells with spire tips ground
off were threaded on two strings of requisite length. The two strings
of shells were laid together so that the shells were in pairs side by side.
Then the strings were laced together with string (worsted in two modern examples), the resulting fabric being a tiny triangular bit of tapestry
between the aperture of each pair of shells, the base of the triangle being
always at the base of the shells. The weft element is continued downward between the next pair of shells to form there the next tiny triangle of tapestry. Each little triangle is secured by a half hitch of
the weft element before it proceeds downward between the next pair
of shells. This half hitch serves also the purpose of throwing the
weft element to the center, where it is hidden from view between the
next two shells. The plate reveals that, although the shells are arranged
aperture to aperture, the lips of the shells of one row always turn down,
the lips of the other row always up, as one looks at one side of the rope.

The short cords which terminate the shell ropes are formed of
tapestry lacing in one example (1-10162) and of three-strand braid in
the other example (plate LXVI). The former rope is nearly twenty-
four feet long.

OLIVE SHELL DISKS

Olive shell disk beads (tunni, C) came from the south as a rule,
though sometimes the Central Miwok made them. Often a southerner
would bring a string of them to a Miwok friend. After drilling the
disks the edges were rubbed smooth on a rock. They were strung on
string, made of either a man's or a woman's hair.

They were measured by the lua (C), that is, the distance from the nipple to the holding thumb and forefinger of the outstretched arm on the opposite side of the body. A lua of olive shell disks was worth five dollars or a fine basket. Their value was only half that of clam shell disks. Brown and white glass beads, obtained from Caucasians, were measured by the lua.

CLAM SHELL BEADS

Clam shell beads (howoku, C), made of *Saxidomus nuttallii,* reached the Central Miwok from the north or northwest and were believed by them to grow thus on the rocks at the ocean shore. Howoku were counted when sold in small numbers. Otherwise the string of howoku was measured, but never by winding around the hand. The unit of measure was the lua. A lua of clam shell beads, about three-eighths of an inch in diameter, was worth ten dollars. At the end of each lua of clam shell disks was placed a large red cylinder, which was white inside. This would seem to have been a glass bead. It was said to come from the ocean, perhaps actually from ships. Possibly it was a magnesite cylinder, such as the Pomo used. A string of large clam shell beads about one inch in diameter, and measuring a motuku ana or half ana (the distance from the middle of the chest to thumb tip of the outstretched arm) was valued at thirty dollars. Why the small sized clam shell beads were measured by the lua and the large sized beads by the half ana is not clear, especially since the two measures are not very different, a lua exceeding a half ana by only a few inches.

One Central Miwok woman living in the mountains, who possessed sixty dollars worth of clam shell disks, was regarded as exceptionally wealthy for that region. She possessed also four abalone pectorals.

Clam shell beads were used as terminal ornaments for wooden ear sticks about three inches long, worn in the lobe of each ear. They were also attached to the headband made of flicker feathers where their whiteness contrasted with the bright color of these feather shafts.

Another object, cylindrical in form, called howobu (C) would appear to be the magnesite cylinder made by the Pomo, judging from the informant's description.

SHELL NOSE-SKEWERS

The cylindrical shell nose-skewer (plate LXIII, fig. 6) came from the south. Among the Central Miwok, according to one appraisal, a fine basket, eight to ten inches in diameter, would be given in exchange for five nose sticks. Another appraisal of their value was much lower, valuing a lua (more than an arm's length) of shell nose-sticks at only two and one-half dollars.

ABALONE PECTORALS

The shell of the red abalone *(Haliotis rufescens)* was obtained at the coast. The Central Miwok designate both the shell and the pectorals made from it as ha'ssunu. Its rough outer layer was ground off and the bright, pearly inner layer cut into pieces for pectorals and other ornaments. A stone saw was said to have been used for the cutting. Pectorals were worn by the chief at fiestas or ceremonial gatherings.

At Knights Ferry in 1923 rectangular pendants were being manufactured by an old man. He was employing modern tools: cleaver, file, and grindstone. These rectangular abalone pieces were worn as pectorals and used as money. Usually six pieces formed a pectoral (tewe, C), or if the pieces were exceptionally large, five sufficed. A set of five large pieces was worth eight or ten dollars, while a set of six smaller pieces was worth six dollars. Anciently a rabbitskin blanket was valued at one pectoral. The Field Museum has some exceptionally large pectorals (70209, 70210) consisting of 17 and 15 disks, respectively, from the mountains of Central Miwok territory. Other pectorals (70213, 70214) from the same place have 19 and 20 smaller disks, respectively.

MEASURES

Strings of shell beads were measured. Beads seem not to have been counted, Pomo fashion. The measures used were (1) lua, from the nipple to the end of the outstretched arm, on the opposite side of the body, the thumb and forefinger holding the beads and marking the end of the measure; (2) ana, the reach from the holding thumb and forefinger of one outstretched arm to the holding thumb and forefinger of the other, usually mentioned as keña ana, one ana; (3) motuku ana, half ana, from the middle of the chest to the holding thumb and finger of one outstretched arm. Other measures for which no names were recorded are (4) from the holding thumb and forefinger to the inside of the elbow joint; (5) from the tip of the middle finger to the wrist joint.

Another unit of measure was the length (stature) of a man. The circular ceremonial earth lodge had a radius of "four men," oyisa yaña (C) and was measured by men lying at full length. The circular brush ceremonial house had a radius of "two and one-half men," otega yaña homotani (C). In this case short men were employed. The "half man" was measured by a man lying on his back with his feet drawn up.

CURRENCY

Shell beads, baskets, acorns, and flicker feather headbands were used as media of exchange. The values of shell beads are discussed elsewhere. Flicker feather headbands were worth about two dollars apiece.

Powers[93] gives some valuations of money: "An Indian is ten days in making a bow, and it is valued at $3, $4, and $5, according to the workmanship; an arrow at 12½ cents. Three kinds of money were employed in this traffic. White shell-buttons, pierced in the center and strung together, rate at $5 a yard (this money was less valuable than among the Nishinam, probably because these lived nearer the source of supply); 'periwinkles' (Olivella?) at $1 a yard; fancy marine shells at various prices, from $3 to $10 or $15 a yard, according to their beauty."

TRADE

The Central Miwok, dwelling in the foothills near Knights Ferry, were in the habit of trading certain seeds for digger pine nuts from people who dwelt somewhat higher in the foothills. Fish taken and dried at Knights Ferry were traded for salt from people still higher in the mountains. The Knights Ferry informant, Louis, had never heard of his people journeying so far into the mountains as Big Trees, Calaveras county. Sugar pine nuts from that region were brought down by other Indians and traded to the Knights Ferry people. Salt from the Mono country on the east side of the Sierra Nevada was brought over by the Eastern Mono in "loaves." These loaves were presented to a Miwok chief to inaugurate the exchange of products.

---

[93]Powers, 352.

He reciprocated with a gift of acorns or other products desired by the Mono. Trade between Miwok and Mono friends was a matter of reciprocal gifts, between Miwok and Mono strangers a matter of bargaining. Yosemite valley, in Southern Miwok territory, was visited by Eastern Mono who brought commodities to trade with the Miwok.

A few rabbit-skin blankets were made by the Central Miwok of Knights Ferry, but the bulk were imported from the Miwok higher in the mountains, who in turn obtained them from the Eastern Mono. Sometimes a Mono would give one to a Miwok friend, who would reciprocate with an arm's length of clam shell beads (howoku, C). Bird skin blankets were unknown at Knights Ferry. Black obsidian (kitcé, C) also came from the mountains, usually in the form of arrowpoints (cawa, C) already made; but sometimes the raw material was brought. A supply was always kept at Knights Ferry, as there were no local substitutes for it. Black was the preferred color for obsidian, but it was described as also coming in red and white.

Shells were obtained from the ocean by the Miwok journeying to the coast for them. Whether this occurred before the coming of the Spaniards is uncertain. At any rate, it was a prevalent custom after the coming of the Spaniards. The shells brought home were worked locally. One Central Miwok woman made a trip to the ocean (polaiau, C) to get shells after the Americans came. However, her prime motive for the trip was to get out of the country after a stabbing affray.

TRAILS

Miwok trails were usually almost airline in their directness, running up hill and down dale without zigzags or detours. Past the soapstone quarry, Lotowayaka, on the north wall of the canyon of the north fork of the Tuolumne river, ran such a trail, connecting the hamlet of Pulayuto, in the meadows east of the north fork of the Tuolumne river, with the hamlet of Hañitwuye, near Soulsbyville. This trail ran straight down one canyon wall and up the other, not zigzagging on the steep slope. On the occasion of festivities at Hañitwuye, the Pulayuto people travelled this trail. The chief of Pulayuto furnished deer for the feast and sometimes his carriers would transport eight or ten deer over this steep trail. The trail was unnamed.

When a stranger was shown over an obscure trail it might be marked for him with sticks thrown down, so that he could find his way back.

In the treeless high Sierra Nevada, Miwok travellers marked their way over the granite wastes with pine needles.

According to Powers,[94] a dead skunk was sometimes hung beside a difficult trail, so that the odor would serve as a guide.

GAMES

We have divided Miwok games into field games and sitting games. In the first category fall shinny, basket ball, ball race, football, foot-cast ball, hoop and pole, lance throwing both with and without a whip, archery contests, and certain children's games such as hide-and-seek and tag. The game in which a lance was thrown by means of a buck-skin thong attached to a stick (Field Museum 70231, 1-3) suggests the Roman method of throwing spears, and also the atlatl, which was used anciently in the Humboldt lake region,[95] Nevada, and which has also been reported from the Santa Barbara region.[96] Of sitting games there were (1) guessing games in which marked and unmarked sticks were hidden in the hands and their positions guessed; (2) stick games in which the number of sticks held were guessed; and (3) dice games.

Men's shinney (alō′la, müla, S) was played by the Southern Miwok on a field similar in size and arrangement to the football field. It was not played by the Central Miwok. Each player was provided with a shinney club of oak or mountain mahogany (mu′la, S), three or four feet long and with a hooked or clubbed end. The Field Museum has a set of four mountain mahogany sticks (70229, 1-4) from Yosemite. The ball (alō′la, S) was about the size and shape of a billiard ball (plate LV, figs. 3, 4), and was made of oak (Field Museum 70233, 1-2), mountain mahogany (Field Museum 70288, 1-2), or mistletoe. Of mistletoe the globose base of the plant was used. This was very hard and cross grained. The game might be played by many men, in which case they lined up as in football. In case only two men played they followed the ball at top speed down the field. The object of each side was to put its ball between the two goal posts. When several men were playing much care was needed in striking the ball so that it would land advantageously to the stroke of the next player in the line. Evidently there were no scrimmages and little danger of injury from

[94]Powers, 351.
[95]Loud and Harrington, 110.
[96]Kroeber, 1925, 560, 816.

an opponent's club. Culin,[97] quoting Hudson, describes the game from two Southern Miwok groups on the Chowchilla river. By the Chowchilla two oak-wood balls, three inches in diameter, were used. "Played only by men, who are divided in two equal sides, say fifteen on a side. The goals, which are each some 200 yards from the center, are two trees or two posts, a long step, or, say, 3 feet, apart. Two men standing side by side cast the ball up and strike it to their opponents' goal." By the Wasama on the Chowchilla river the game was called "müla". Dr. Hudson describes it as follows: "Played with a club, mu-lau' of mountain mahogany, and a mahogany ball, o-lo'-la.

"Two or more men play in couples or pairs from a start line (fig. 812). The captains at station 1 strike their respective balls toward their respective partners at station 2. If the ball falls short of 2, the failing striker must forward his ball to station 2 by an additional stroke; when the ball passes into the territory of the partner at station 2, he (no. 2) must drive it forward from where it stopped. The last stationed partner must drive it over the goal line. The smallest number of aggregate strokes on a side wins. Station keepers must keep within their own territories."

The women's shinney game (ti'klī, P, N, C) was played on a field quite similar to that of the men's. It was played with sharp-pointed, five-foot, willow poles and with a rope ring two feet in diameter or with a braided buckskin string (modernly a rag) a foot and a half to three feet long. In the center of the field was a small shallow hole into which, at a given signal, a man threw the ring or string. Immediately the women scrambled for possession of it and each endeavored to throw it toward her end of the field. It could not be carried on the stick and must not be touched by the hand. In the scramble a woman would sometimes have her foot jabbed by a stick accidentally. Any desired number of women might engage in the game. Among some of the Miwok there was but one goal post, some six feet in height, at each end of the field. The string or ring must be thrown against a goal post to score. In this respect the game resembles the lacrosse game of eastern North America. One Central Miwok informant stated that in the form she knew the game there were two goals of arched willow branches about one hundred yards apart. The endeavor was to drive the ring or string to the opponents' end of the field and over

---

[97] 631.

their goal. There was no special grouping of players by lineage or moiety, but often people of different localities played against one another. Each side staked valuables. One informant stated the game and the name ti'klī were Maidu and acquired directly from that people. Dr. Hudson records,[98] under the name "tawilu" (S). what appears to be a form of this game. "Two or more women contest with 3-foot sticks for a braided buckskin strip 10 inches long. The goals are 150 feet apart."

Basket ball. This game, called a'mta (P, N, C) and ama'tʉp (C), was played by women and girls only. The field was about two hundred yards long and had a willow arch goal at each end, or else two upright posts at each end, as shown in text-figure 86. A single ball, called po'sko (P, N, C), about two and a half inches in diameter, was employed, and each woman was furnished with a pair of handled baskets resembling seed beaters and called ama"ta (P), tcama'tī (N), a'mta and ammutna (C). These and two of the balls used in this game are shown in plate LV, figs. 1, 2, 5, 6. The ball was of buckskin stuffed with deer hair, moss, or grass. A man, called the potcukbe (C), tnrew the single ball down hard in the middle of the field. Then the women who were in their positions on each side rushed and scrambled for it. The attempt was made to catch it when it bounced. It could be caught only in the baskets, being caught in the larger of the two baskets and covered with the smaller, while the player ran. If caught with the hands the side having the ball had to give it up, and a game was counted lost by that side. Each side tried to carry it or throw it through its own goal, past the line of opponents standing there, who tackled the players who carried the ball, and if possible threw the ball back toward their own goal. The group, which put the ball between its own goal posts first, won. Male and female spectators as well as the players bet on the outcome. All sorts of property were wagered, including horses and money in later days. At times water moiety women played against land moiety women, but there seems to have been no alignments on the basis of lineages. Culin[99] describes the rackets used in this game only for the Central Miwok (Bald Rock and Groveland, Tuolumne county). He pictures three baskets and a ball. Culin describes this game as football rather than basket ball and states that equal numbers of men and

---

[98]Culin, 659.
[99]596, 597.

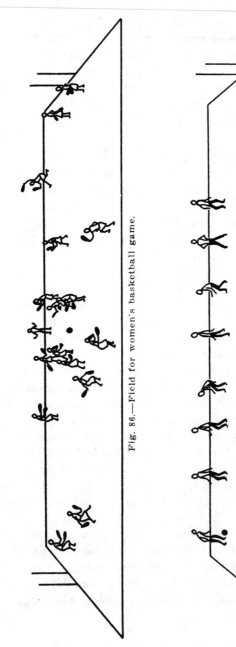

Fig. 86.—Field for women's basketball game.

Fig. 87.—Field for men's football game.

women played, the former kicking the ball, the latter carrying it with their baskets.[100]

Culin,[101] after quoting Hudson, describes for the Central Miwok, under the name "sakumship" a basket ball game in which no men partici-pate: "Two women, standing 50 feet apart, throw a 4-inch ball of buckskin filled with hair, each using two baskets to throw the ball, which they may not touch with their hands. The casting baskets, called shak-num-sia, are made somewhat stronger than the a-ma-ta.

"This is a great gambling game between women, and is played for high stakes. It is counted with sticks, and a player forfeits one if she fails to catch or throw the ball so that it goes beyond the other's reach."

A sort of lacrosse game was played by the Central Miwok with a buckskin ball three or four inches in diameter. The players tried to put the ball through a triangular opening at the top of the goal stick about ten feet above ground. The ball was caught and thrown in a small basket on a stick. Several men might play on each side. This may be the game described by Bancroft.[102]

Ball race. Culin[103] describes a ball race as played about 1850 by the Cosumni, a Plains Miwok group. Two parallel tracks were laid off and each party had its own ball. The game was more properly a foot race.

Culin also mentions the game from the Southern Miwok, called the Wasama, near Grant Springs, Mariposa county.

Football. This game, called po'sko (P, N, C) was played by men or boys only. The field and the initial positions of the players are shown in text-figure 87. The field was usually about fifty yards long and had only one pair of goal posts, six to eight feet apart, set up at one end. The players, sometimes as many as twenty-five on a side, ranged themselves down the length of the field, and each group so manoeuvered its ball as to send it between the goal posts. The two balls, also called po'sko (P, N), (plate LV, figs. 5, 6), were placed each on a little cone of earth about six inches in height, and were kicked off at a given signal. The skill in this game lay in so kicking the ball that it would fall advantageously for the next player in the line to kick it toward the goal. The spectators on the side lines held the stakes

---

[100]Culin, 703, 597; fig. 919.
[101]597.
[102]Bancroft, 393.
[103]669-670.

and served as judges. No umpire or referee was needed and in case of any difference of opinion among the players the spectators settled the matter. No player was allowed to touch the ball with his hands while it was in motion. The ball used in this game was six or eight inches in diameter and was made of buckskin filled with deer hair, shredded cedar bark, moss, or soaproot fiber. Culin, after Hudson, describes this game for the Central Miwok.[104] He states that the field was five hundred yards long, whereas our informant said fifty yards. It would seem likely that his figure is the more correct one, though Culin does add that the number of players regulates the length of the field.

A variant of the football game just described is called wī'topup or wī'tupo (C). It employed two goals like those in the women's basket ball game (amta, C). Two balls, eight to ten inches in diameter, were kicked by men of the opposing teams simultaneously. Each side tried to get its ball through the goal first. Once this was accomplished they turned and repeated the performance to the other goal. Neither goal was owned by either side. Bets were collected after each play to one end of the field.

Perhaps a variant of this game, also Central Miwok, was one in which footballs of buckskin or modernly of rags, were kicked the length of a field, one by each of several players. The starting point was two poles about eight feet apart. Each man tried to kick his ball first through the goal posts, also about eight feet apart and about a quarter mile distant.

Foot-cast ball. Culin[105] reports "a game of casting a heavy stone ball with the top of the foot, the object being to see who can throw it farthest; observed only in California by Doctor Hudson among the tribes of two stocks (Mariposan and Moquelumnan)." For the Miwok (Moquelumnan) he reports the game from Aplache, Big Creek, north of Groveland, Tuolumne county, California. The Aplache people at Groveland were of Southern Miwok lineage, so the game evidently should be attributed to the Southern Miwok. Central Miwok informants did not know the game. Its Southern Miwok attribution is strengthened by its presence among the Chukchansi. The game was called by the Aplache "sawa puchuma (sawa, stone; puchuma, to lift

---

[104]702.
[105]711, 712.

or cast with the top of the foot) : A pecked stone ball, about 3 inches in diameter, is cast with the top of the right foot. The left foot must not get out of position. The one who can throw it farthest wins."

Hoop and pole game. The ring and dart game (te'ūle, C) was played by the Central Miwok. A ring about a foot in diameter was made of chaparral, or of wild cherry *(Prunus demissa),* and wound with buckskin. This was rolled along a course by one of the players and his opponent threw a five-foot dart, hū'la (C), at the ring as it approached him edge on. If he put the dart through the ring, the roller must give him a dart and allow him another trial. Thus they played until all the darts were in the possession of one player. No betting was done on this game as a rule. It was played by children, chiefly boys, and by women, more than by men.

For the Central Miwok near Groveland, Tuolumne county, Culin has published Hudson's description of the game[106] under the name "teweknumsia" :

"The implements consist of a plain lance, ho-cha, 10 feet in length, marked on the butt end with proprietary marks, in paint, and a hoop of oak, 30 inches in diameter, bound with buckskin, te-wek-num-sia. The game is played by four players, who face each other on opposite sides of a square 90 feet across. The casters, each of whom have four lances, stand opposite to each other, while two assistants, one for each side, roll the hoop across. As the wheel rolls, both casters throw at it, each trying to transfix it. If one is successful his opponent comes across to his place, and, standing in the successful caster's tracks, tries to transfix the fallen hoop. After him, the first player tries at the same mark and from the same position. They cast alternately until all have thrown their four lances. The greater number of transfixing spears decides. There are 30 counting-sticks, 15 to a side. The buckskin is to keep the hoop from bounding."

For the Southern Miwok, Culin,[107] quoting Hudson, records the game from the Chowchilla river, where it was known as "pachitu" : "A ring of Asclepias, 2½ inches in diameter, called he-wi'-ta, is rolled, the caster racing, and casting after the ring a 10-foot lance, called hu-wo'-ta. A 'lean' counts 3, a 'balance' 5, and a 'transfix' 12."

The Field Museum of Natural History possesses two sets of four

---

[106]Culin, 484.
[107]484.

lances each (70234, 1-4; 70235, 1-4) of wild cherry *(Prunus demissa)*. These are about nine feet long, peeled only at the ends, and pointed at the distal end. The specimens are from Groveland in Central Miwok territory.

From the Southern Miwok group known as Wasama, in Madera county, Culin, quoting Hudson, describes a variant game in which arrows are shot at the hoop, made of *Fremontia californica* bark bound with buckskin.[108] This game was called "hewitu numhe."

Lance throwing. Culin,[109] after Hudson, describes two forms of lance throwing observed among the Central Miwok near Groveland, Tuolumne county. In one, four-foot lances of decorticated willow or *Calacanthus* were cast along the ground. The player throwing farthest won. The loser was thumped on the head with the knuckles. The game was called "pakumship," after "pakür, lance."

The second form was one in which the lance, thirty-eight inches in length, was thrown with a whip consisting of a thirty-one inch rod with a buckskin thong attached. The game was called "kuitumsi (kuitu, farthest one)." The lance was called "lamakuyita," the buckskin thong "pehunahaata (buckskin to whip)." The farthest cast won. The Field Museum has a whip and two lances (70231, 1-3), which are figured by Culin (figure 535).

Archery contest. Culin[110] describes, after Hudson, an archery game played by the Central Miwok of the vicinity of Groveland. The name of the game was recorded as "thuyamship." "The two contestants, armed with bows and blunt arrows, stand beside an arrow stuck in the ground and shoot alternately from a distance of about 170 feet. Two other players stand near the arrow targets and mark the shots. The players shoot back and forth until one of the two arrow targets is struck and broken." The Field Museum has two arrows (70243, 1-2) collected in Yosemite valley in 1857, and said to have been used in a game.

CHILDREN'S GAMES

Four children's games were recorded among the Central Miwok. One was a guessing game, upon which the children bet. The others were of a more active character.

---

[108]Culin, 485.
[109]414, 415.
[110]388.

Kusta (C). The guessing game was played by either boys or girls. A bit of charcoal was held in the two doubled fists, then hidden in one, and the arms folded. The opponents guessed in which hand the charcoal was held. Twelve sticks were employed for tally. Several children played on each side. One hid the charcoal in his hand. If he won he passed it to a partner. If he lost he passed it to the opposing side. This game is perhaps to be equated to a Southern Miwok game "called hu'-sa, in which one guesses which hand hides a hidden seed or nut."[111] Hudson, whom Culin quotes, does not state if this was a children's game.

Ululu (C). A band of girls and boys formed a long line and made a wide circuit. First one sang and they turned in his direction; perhaps he would be at the end. Then another sang, perhaps in the middle. Then the hind and front ones tried to find him.

Onomu (C) was hide-and-seek, much as played by white children. The seekers (likuti, C) called out in a peculiar way. They hid their faces to give the hider a chance to secrete himself. The hider called out when the search failed. The last searcher to return had to be the hider. If the hider was found, he hid again.

Senuyu (C) was last tag. When playing children went home they "last tagged" each other. A "last tagged" person must not look at the tagger.

Playing children threw the stems of the rattlesnake weed, *Daucus pusillus* (yotcitayu, C), at one another, as the seeds adhere to clothing and hair.

SITTING GAMES

A number of games were played seated, either outdoors or indoors. These were guessing games and dice games, and were always the basis of wagers.

Hand game or *grass game*. As played by men this game, called a'lle (P), hī'nᴜwa or hī'nᴜwo (N), hīno'wū (C), and hinawu (S), required two pairs of bones, each bone being about the size of a man's first finger. One of each pair was grooved and snugly wrapped, usually about its middle, with blackened string or sinew, and was called uѕu'u (P); o'ssa (N), "woman;" tiyauni (S). The unwrapped bone was

---
[111]Culin, 294.

called sa'uwe (P), and na'ña (N, S), "man." The pair, a wrapped and an unwrapped bone, was called ha'na (P, N, C), and pa'tu (C). Such ones are shown in plate LVII, figs. 9-14, and plate LXXI, figs. 1 and 2. Culin figures three sets from the Central Miwok.[112] Two of these sets are of tubular bones filled with slender twigs. In the set numbered 70216 (Field Museum), Culin's figure 383, the two with buckskin winding also have this material passing inside the tube. 70216-3 is 95 mm. long.

In playing, these bones were hidden in bunches of green grass or pine needles, and the opposite side must guess in which hand the un-marked bone[113] was concealed. Ten counters (kü'tca, P, N; hï'llo, C; huhu, S) were used, which were small sticks, eight to twelve inches long. Culin describes a Central Miwok set of ten sticks (Field Museum 70232) of peeled wild cherry *(Prunus demissa)* sharpened at one end, and fifteen inches in length.[114] There were two men on each side who hid the bones, though anyone was privileged to bet on the game. A pair of the bones was used by each of the two players on the side whose turn it was to hide the bones. They hid the bones in bunches of grass or pine needles, rolling these around in time to their gambling song (hi'nūwo, C), which was supposed to bring them good luck and confuse their opponents. When ready for the guessing by the oppo-nents, this pair of players held their closed hands in front of their chests and revolved one about the other, in time to their song, until the guess was made. If the guess was incorrect the holders retained the bones for another round and received as many counters as there were points lost by the guessers' side. If both were guessed right the guessers received two counters and had the next play. If only one was guessed right the guessers received one counter and the player incorrectly guessed had another play.

At the outset the ten counters were held by a tally keeper or stake holder, who received a small percentage of the stakes for his services and who was the only person not privileged to bet on the game. During the first stages of the game he distributed the counters as won, until all ten were gone. Thereafter the counters were passed directly from side to side, until one side had all ten and the game was finished.

---

[112]Figs. 383-385.
[113]According to two Central Miwok informants, it was always the marked bone that was sought by both men and women players. Probably the custom varied. In fact, another Central Miwok informant called the marked stick "man", the unmarked "woman", and said it was the "woman" which was sought.
[114]Culin, 295.

The several possibilities in this guessing are indicated in the following table, in which X indicates the marked and O the unmarked bones, R the right hands and L the left hands of a pair of players:

R	L	R	L
X	O	X	O
X	O	O	X
O	X	O	X
O	X	X	O
OX		OX	
	OX		OX
OX			OX
	OX	OX	

The women's hand game (welĕ'yūp, hinwo, C) was played by four women, two on each side. Each pair of bones was called a "man" (unmarked bone) and a "woman" (marked bone), the latter being sought. The bones were of deer leg bone usually, though mountain lion leg bone was preferred. Culin figures a set made of split mountain lion femur.[115] Twelve stick counters were placed in the middle of the game area at the start. These were paid out by the male umpire (hilukbe, C). When these had been distributed between the two sides, the game continued until one side had won all the counters. Both players who had the bones participated in the hiding, while one person in the opposing pair guessed their location, often after consulting her partner. In shuffling the bones the women's hands were hidden under a piece of buckskin or behind their heads. Then the arms were folded so that each hand was hidden in an armpit. If the location of both marked bones was guessed, two counters passed to the guesser's side. If only one was guessed, one counter was passed to the guesser's side. If two were correctly guessed, the winners had the next play. If only one was guessed, the one missed played again. If she were afraid that she might be correctly guessed, she might pass the play to her partner. It did not matter which of the opposing pair guessed. Singing of the contestants continually accompanied the playing.

Informants stated that hand-game songs were different from songs generally in use among the Miwok, and that they came from the tribes living to the west, particularly about San Jose.

---

[115]Fig. 385.

Stick game. This game (o'lūtca, C) was played by men only and with forty-four small sticks. One player held the bunch of sticks in his left hand and suddenly separated a bunch of them in his right. He placed this hand behind his back and his opponent guessed one, two, three, or four. The sticks were then counted in fours and any remainder noted. If the remainder was the figure named by the guesser, he received the bundle of sticks: if not, he lost his bet. The terms used in guessing were: ken, one; os, two; tule'k, three; to, four (C). It is to be noted that these are not the full names of the numerals.

Another form of this game (yü'tto, P, N) was played by the Plains and Northern Miwok. Ten wormwood rods, each eight to ten inches in length, were held by each of the two players in his left hand. The one sang his gambling song and suddenly separated a number of sticks in his right hand. His opponent must then guess whether this was an odd number (tele'ka, P, N) or an even number. If the guess was correct the guessing changed sides; if not, the guesser gave his opponent one of the ten counters (kü'ttca, P, N), used in keeping the tally. Virtually the same game, called olatc*u'* (C) was played by Central Miwok men with eight sticks, each a foot long and about the diameter of a lead pencil.

Dice game. A dice game (hele'lla, P, N; ha'h*u*, N; tca'тa, tcaтa'tu, or hahumetitci, C) was played with halves of acorn meats (plate LXX, figs. 7, 8), half walnuts (plate LXXI, figs. 4, 5), or half cylinders of wood, chiefly by women. The half acorns were not colored, but the wooden dice, an inch and a half or two inches in length, were darkened on the rounded surface. Four (sometimes six or eight) dice were shaken in the cupped hands and released suddenly, often with a slight swinging motion, being dropped on a mat or upon a flat, coiled basketry tray (hetalu, C). A tray in the Field Museum (70221) is 510 mm. in diameter and is from Groveland. It has a zigzag design.

Either two or four persons played this game. Eight, ten, or twelve counters (hĭ'lo, C) were used in tallying. At the start of the game the counters were placed centrally between the players. The game was won when all counters were in possession of either side. They then appropriated the valuables which had been staked by their opponents. The scores counted as follows: if all flat or all rounded sides turned up, two points; if an equal number of flat and rounded sides, one point.

Any other combination counted nothing. Woman versus woman or man versus woman, but never man versus man was the rule.

Culin[116] reports this game, with six dice, among the Southern Miwok (the Awani, near Cold Springs, Mariposa county), under the name "teatacu." He figures a basket plaque, nearly twenty-four inches in diameter (figure 162) used for this game.

Northern Miwok specimen 1-10035 comprises four acorn dice, the only form originally used with a flat basket tray.

Game of staves. The game of staves, mū'ltūya (C), was played by women. Six staves about eight inches in length and semi-circular in cross-section were cast upon a piece of matting or deer skin. The score was counted as with the dice. If all fell with the rounded side up or all with the flat side up, two points were scored. If they were evenly divided one point was scored. Any other combination did not count. Ten counters (hī'lo, C) were used as in the dice game. This was a gambling game, but was sometimes played without bets.

TOYS

The chief toys of children were made from acorns. Apparently there were local difference in the acorn toys. Southern informants were not acquainted with the acorn musical string of the north. The Northern Miwok did not use the acorn top of the south.

The acorn musical string (kō'wa, P, N) consisted of acorns strung on an ordinary string. By holding the string so that one of these acorns struck lightly against the upper incisors when the remainder of the acorns on the string were whirled, a peculiar sound was produced. This might be modified by changing the form of the buccal cavity. This instrument was also employed to some extent by adults. See plate LXX, figs. 1 and 2.

The acorn top (lutu'nna, C) is shown in plate LXX, figs. 4-6. This was almost exclusively a child's toy and no game was played with it.

An acorn buzzer toy called luma'a (C) resembled the toy known among white children as the buzz saw. As is shown in plate LXX, fig. 3, it consisted simply of an acorn perforated near its middle by two holes, through which a double cord was passed. By twisting these cords and then exerting a slight tension at intervals, the acorn was made to spin like a buzz saw.

---

[116] 143.

Miwok children had a whistle (sūle'pa, P, N), composed of a section of goose quill with a small hole burned into its side.

Toy bows and arrows were made for boys.

Dolls were made of shredded soaproot leaves, tied on sticks, and folded over the end of a stick to make a head. No cradle was made, but a pine spindle house was constructed for the doll. This was furnished with a bed of pine needles.

CAT'S CRADLE

Cat's cradle was called umasi' (C). Eight forms were observed and recorded by photographing. They are shown in plates LXVII-LXIX. The various things represented were (1) the sky, clear and cloudy; (2) the flea, still and jumping; (3) stealing; (4) gopher; (5) boy baby; (6) girl baby; (7) fish net; (8) bark house. The eighth form has been noted by Gifford among the Cocopa, who designated it "willow roots," and among the Kamia, who designated it "fox nose."

LOVE CHARMS

No information was obtained from informants as to such objects. Specimen 15-5819, Museum of the American Indian, Heye Foundation, is a modern object from Yosemite valley, and is reputed to be a love charm. It consists of a necklace composed of six toes, probably cottontail rabbit toes, with fur and claws. The toes are separated by pieces of whitish root cut as beads. Between each two toes are two to four pieces of root.

DOGS

The ancient dog (tcuku, C) of the Miwok was brindled, medium-sized, prick-eared, short-haired, had a curled tail, and a muzzle like a coyote. Dogs were rare and were usually bought as pups from the westerners (Alowituk), probably the Yokuts. Sometimes, however, they were bred by the Miwok. Pups were bought with baskets, bows, and arrows. The dogs sometimes caught squirrels. Hunters sometimes used the dogs for pursuing deer, which the dogs could run down easily in the fall when the deer were fat. Also wounded deer were run down by dogs.

Dogs were sometimes eaten. They were commonly named after their owner's homeland. The father of one aged informant possessed a bitch (tcuku osa, C) which he named Sokonowa after a place near his native hamlet of Akanga. Sokonowa was an esteemed member of the household who slept next the fire. Her master never hunted with her, but kept her as a valuable piece of property. Sokonowa was never mated by her owner, although there were several other dogs in the village. He had obtained her while living at the upcountry village of Pota (near Springfield, Tuolumne county), his brothers dwelling at Akanga having got her from the Yokuts for him. Sokonowa died of old age, having escaped the end of so many Miwok dogs who were shot on the occasion of the pota or pole ceremony.

THE CULTURAL POSITION OF THE SIERRA MIWOK

To the south the Yokuts seem to have been far more influenced by Great Basin Shoshonean culture than the Miwok. Perhaps this was because the Shoshonean Western Mono lived on the western slope of the Sierra Nevada in contact with the Yokuts and thus formed a channel through which Great Basin Shoshonean traits flowed to the Yokuts. The Miwok, on the other hand, had no constant contact with Shoshoneans along their eastern border, being separated from them by the high Sierra, which can be crossed only in summer. This mountain barrier was no doubt an important factor in hindering the Miwok absorption of Great Basin cultural traits. The Ghost Dance cults of 1870 and 1890 are cases in point. The influence of the 1870 form did not reach the Miwok direct from its Paiute originators to the east, but only through the medium of central Californian people to the west.[117]

In food habits the Miwok seem typical of the central Californian culture area. This is pretty clearly set off from the northwestern Californian area by the abstention in the latter area from the eating of dogs, reptiles, and insects. Southern California, except the Colorado River region, cannot be differentiated upon such a basis, the southerners being as omnivorous as the central peoples. What differences there are between central and southern peoples are largely due to floral and faunal environment. Dog eating has a south central and southern Californian distribution and suggests the possibility of Mexican influence.

---

[117]Gifford, 1926, 400.

Kroeber states[118] that seines, gill nets, and dip nets were probably known to all Californians, but that their use or non-use was dependent on local fishing conditions. This is well illustrated by the Miwok use of nets: seines in the still, broad reaches of water, set gill nets in the streams, and dip nets for deep holes. The casting net, suggesting that of the Polynesians, was used by the Plains Miwok and seems to have been reported nowhere else in California.

From the regions of the Northern, Central, and Southern Miwok come scattering archaeological specimens, including the famous "finds" from the auriferous gravels, once regarded as evidence of the existence of man in early Tertiary times. The types of auriferous gravel artifacts have been pictured and described, and their probable Indian origin indicated.[119] The portable bowl mortar is conspicuous among them. The Miwok attribute to it a supernatural origin, imputing its invention usually to Coyote. The historic type of mortar for acorn pounding is the bedrock mortar.

What brought about the change from portable bowl to stationary bedrock mortars is not known. The hypothesis suggests itself, however, that the seasonal movements to higher and lower altitudes may have led to the invention of the bedrock mortar as a temporary convenience. Transportation of the heavy portable mortars, often weighing a hundred pounds, would have been a difficult and wasteful proceeding, when the available transport was needed for the food products gathered. Thus the bedrock mortar may gradually have come into use. The bedrock mortar is formed by use and does not have to be laboriously pecked out as do the finished portable mortars. This fact may have led to the gradual abandonment of the portable mortar. Moreover the bedrock mortars served a social purpose. Those for a hamlet were often all situated in a single granite outcrop. This meant that the matrons gathered there, instead of each preparing her acorns separately at home in a portable mortar.

In certain respects some Miwok objects display crudeness in comparison with the corresponding objects of their neighbors, as the following examples demonstrate:

(1) Miwok bone sticks for the hand game are crude sections of bone cut squarely off at each end (plate LVII, figs. 9-14). From the

---

[118]1925, 816.
[119]Holmes, 1901, 419-472.

Washo the Miwok obtained an elliptical type, finely finished, and with the black central wrapping let into the bone to give added smoothness (plate LXXI, fig. 1).

(2)   The best Miwok basketry is not so fine as the best basketry of neighboring tribes, to-wit: Washo, Mono, Yokuts, and Maidu. This applies both to coiling and twining. For example, Maidu, Washo, and Mono burden baskets for seeds are patterned and tightly woven, while the corresponding Miwok receptacle is an openwork one with the interstices closed with a coating of soaproot juice, which hardens to a glue-like consistency. The Miwok twined trays are crude openwork affairs. The Washo and Mono make tightly woven, patterned ones. The absence of feathered basketry in Miwok collections contrasts with its presence in Yokuts collections.

(3)   In using the whole olive shell for necklaces instead of cutting it into perforated disks or squares, the Miwok dwelling in the mountains correspond to the primitive Coast Yuki, who, although living on the shores where the shells were found, never developed any form of beads other than the whole shell.[120] The Miwok acquired olive-shell disk beads from their neighbors, but never advanced to their manufacture. Similarly, clam-shell beads were not made by the Miwok of the hills and mountains, but perhaps were made by the Plains Miwok in whose territory huge quantities have been unearthed from aboriginal sites.

Whole olive shells were used by the ancient people of Lovelock cave in the same general way as among the mountain Miwok, namely, by making into long ropes of parallel rows of shells. The manner of attachment of the shells was somewhat more intricate than among the Miwok.[121]

(4)   The feather dance skirts of the Miwok resemble those of the Maidu. But in the technique of attaching the feathers the Miwok were less skillful than the Maidu. Both cut the base of the quill to resemble the point of a quill pen. This was folded over the string of the net to which it was to be attached. The Maidu inserted the point of the quill into its shaft.[122] The Miwok merely folded it over and lashed it with string.

---

[120]Gifford, 1928, 114.
[121]Loud and Harrington, fig. 17; pl. 53.
[122]Dixon, 1905, fig. 24.

(5)   In northern California a slab of stone is used as a mortar. Upon it was placed a bottomless flaring basket hopper to prevent the fragments of acorn scattering when struck by the pestle. Among the Miwok the basket hopper was unknown, even though it would have been very serviceable with the shallower depressions of the bedrock mortars. The acorn fragments which flew off with each stroke of the pestle were retrieved instead with a soaproot brush.

(6)   The manufacture of carved oaken bowls among none of the Miwok, except the Southern, and their manufacture among the Western Mono, are significant.

(7)   The wooden tobacco pipes of the three divisions of Sierra Miwok were at best crude affairs. The elderberry pipe was the easiest made and simplest type of tobacco pipe. The superiority of workmanship in the pipes of their neighbors immediately to the south is shown in plate LVI, figs. 5-12.

(8)   Crude coiled pottery was made by certain Yokuts and Mono groups. Its manufacture never extended to the Miwok.

(9)   Except for rare examples from east of the Sierra Nevada, the metate was not used by the Miwok. The mortar was employed for all sorts of seeds.

In short, although the dwellers of the delta region (among whom some Plains Miwok were doubtless included) had one of the richest cultures of central California, the Sierra Miwok were relatively primitive in culture. This situation conforms to what is generally observable in California; namely, that valley dwellers have a richer culture than mountain dwellers.

BIBLIOGRAPHY

Abbreviations: AMNH-B, American Museum of Natural History Bulletin; BAE-B, Bureau of American Ethnology Bulletin; BAE-R, Bureau of American Ethnology Annual Report; UC-PAAE, University of California Publications in American Archaeology and Ethnology; UC-PG, University of California Publications in Geography.

Bancroft, H. H.
  1875. The Native Races of the Pacific States of North America. 1, Wild Tribes. New York: D. Appleton and Company.

Barrett, S. A.
  1908. The Geography and Dialects of the Miwok Indians. UC-PAAE 6:333-380.
  1910. The Material Culture of the Klamath Lake and Modoc Indians of Northeastern California and Southern Oregon. UC-PAAE 5:239-292.
  1916. Pomo Buildings. Holmes Anniversary Volume:1-17. Washington, D. C.
  1917. The Washo Indians. Bulletin of the Milwaukee Public Museum 2:1-52.

Chesnut, V. K.
  1902. Plants used by the Indians of Mendocino County, California. Contrib. U. S. National Herbarium 7: No. 3.

Culin, Stewart
  1907. Games of the North American Indians. BAE-R 24.

Dixon, Roland B.
  1905. The Northern Maidu. AMNH-B 17:119-346.
  1907. The Shasta. AMNH-B 17:381-498.

Dorsey, George A.
  1903. Indians of the Southwest. Passenger Department, Atchison, Topeka and Santa Fe Railway System.

Eakle, Arthur S.
  1923. Minerals of California. California State Mining Bureau, Bull. 91.

Gifford, E. W.
  1917. Miwok Myths. UC-PAAE 12:283-338.
  1926. Miwok Cults. UC-PAAE 18:391-408.

1928. The Cultural Position of the Coast Yuki. Am. Anthr., n.s., 30:112-115.

1932. The Northfork Mono. UC-PAAE 31:15-65.

Grinnell, Joseph, and Storer, Tracy Irwin.

1921. Life Zones of the Yosemite Region. *In* Handbook of Yosemite National Park, compiled and edited by Ansel F. Hall. G. P. Putnam's Sons, New York.

1924. Animal Life in the Yosemite. Contribution from the Museum of Vertebrate Zoology, University of California.

Holmes, W. H.

1901. Review of Evidence Relating to Auriferous Gravel Man in California. Smithsonian Report for 1899. :419-472.

1902. Anthropological Studies in California. Report U. S. Nat. Mus. for 1900:155-188.

Jepson, Willis Linn.

1910. The Silva of California. Memoirs of the University of California 2.

1921. The Giant Sequoia. *In* Handbook of Yosemite National Park.

Krause, Fritz.

1921. Die Kultur der kalifornischen Indianer. Staatliche Forschungsinstitute in Leipzig, Institut für Völkerkunde, Erste Reihe: Ethnographie und Ethnologie 4.

Kroeber, A. L.

1908. On the Evidences of the Occupation of Certain Regions by the Miwok Indians. UC-PAAE 6:369-380.

1925. Handbook of the Indians of California. BAE-B 78.

1929. The Valley Nisenan. UC-PAAE 24:253-290.

Loud, L. L., and Harrington, M. R.

1929. Lovelock Cave. UC-PAAE 25:1-183.

Merriam, C. Hart.

1907. Distribution and Classification of the Mewan Stock of California. Amer. Anthr., n.s., 9:338-357.

1914. Distribution of Indian tribes in the southern Sierra and adjacent parts of the San Joaquin valley, California. Science, n.s., 19:912-917.

1926. The Buffalo in Northeastern California. Journal of Mammalogy 7:211-214.

Merrill, Ruth Earl.
   1923. Plants used in Basketry by the California Indians. UC-
      PAAE 20:215-242.
Powers, Stephen.
   1877. Tribes of California. Contrib. N. Am. Ethn. 3, Washington.
Russell, Richard Joel.
   1926. Climates of California. UC-PG 2:73-84.
Schenck, W. Egbert, and Dawson, Elmer J.
   1929. Archaeology of the Northern San Joaquin Valley. UC-
      PAAE 25:289-413.
Setchell, William Albert.
   1921. Aboriginal Tobaccos. Am. Anthr., n.s., 23:397-414.
Sparkman, Philip Stedman.
   1908. The Culture of the Luiseño Indians. UC-PAAE 8:187-234.
Wissler, Clark.
   1922. The American Indian, 2nd edition. New York: Oxford Uni-
      versity Press.

EXPLANATION OF PLATE XXVIII.

Figure 1. Typical foot-hill region of the Sierra Nevada, in Central Miwok territory. Neg. No. 5559.

Figure 2. The Sierra Nevada of 3,000 to 4,000 feet elevation in Central Miwok territory. Neg. No. 5557.

1

2

EXPLANATION OF PLATE XXIX.

Figure 1. The higher Sierra Nevada region, visited only in summer by the Miwok. Vernal and Nevada falls with the snow-clad summits of the high Sierra in the background. Yosemite Valley lies immediately adjacent, to the left. M.P.M. Neg. No. 406395.

Figure 2. Site of the village of Eyeyaku, near Tuolumne. Altitude about 2,600 feet. Village site in background, bedrock mortar in foreground, Turnback creek between site and bedrock. Neg. No. 7125.

1

2

EXPLANATION OF PLATE XXX.

Figure 1. Handling hot cooking stones with the wooden tongs, Northern Miwok, Railroad Flat, Calaveras County. Neg. No. 2739.

Figure 2. Entrance to the conical slab grinding house. Within may be seen the portable stone mortar. In the doorway are several cobblestone pestles, Northern Miwok, Railroad Flat, Calaveras County. Neg. No. 2755.

1

2

EXPLANATION OF PLATE XXXI.

Figures 1-4. Wooden paddles for stirring acorn mush and other foods while cooking. Specimen Nos. 1-10070 (C), 1-9963 (N), 1-10126 (C), 1-10287 (C). Fig. 2 measures 1008 mm. Neg. No. 2775.

Figure 5. Looped stirring stick for lifting hot cooking stones from baskets. Specimen No. 1-10331 (S). Neg. No. 2775.

Figures 6, 7. Wooden fire tongs for handling hot cooking stones. Specimen No. 1-9964 (N). Neg. No. 2775.

Figure 8. Two large acorn granaries, Railroad Flat, Calaveras County. Northern Miwok. Neg. No. 2751.

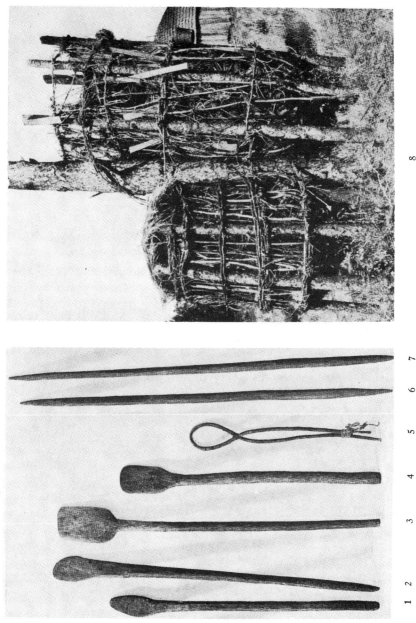

285

EXPLANATION OF PLATE XXXII.

Figures 1–4.   Cooking stones used in boiling in baskets.   Spec. No. 1-10061 (N).   Neg. No. 5976.

Figure   5.   Stone pestle, unusually well formed.   Length 380 mm. Spec. No. 1-9940 (N).   Neg. No. 5967.

Figure   6.   Stone acorn cracker.   Spec. No. 1-10010 (N).   Neg. No. 5967.

Figure   7.   Stone pestle.   Spec. No. 1-10087 (C).   Neg. No. 5967.

Figure   8.   Stone pestle, unusually well formed.   Spec. No. 1-10085 (C).   Neg. No. 5969.

Figure   9.   Steatite dish, very roughly formed.   Spec. No. 1-10506 (N).   Neg. No. 5969.

Figure   10.   Cylindrical stone pestle.   Length 322 mm.   Spec. No. 1-10316 (C).   Neg. No. 5969.

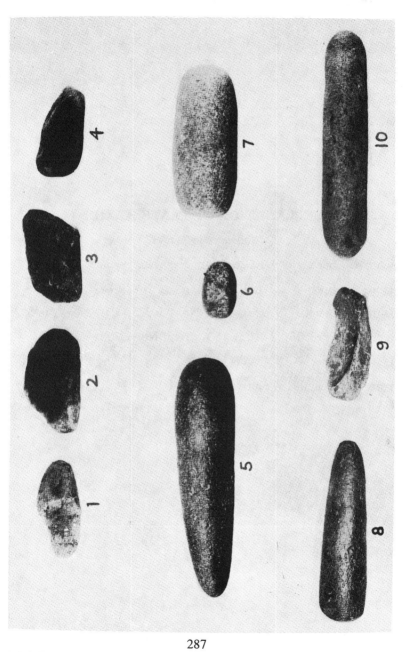

287

EXPLANATION OF PLATE XXXIII.

Cobblestone pestles.

Figure 1. Spec. No. 1-10326 (C). Neg. No. 5975.

Figure 2. Spec. No. 1-10017 (N). Neg. No. 5975.

Figure 3. Length 207 mm. Spec. No. 1-10325 (C). Neg. No. 5975.

Figure 4. Spec. No. 1-10251 (S). Neg. No. 5979.

Figure 5. Spec. No. 1-10253 (S). Neg. No. 5979.

Figure 6. Length 184 mm. Spec. No. 1-10324 (C). Neg. No. 5979.

EXPLANATION OF PLATE XXXIV.

Globose stone mortar.   Height 210 mm.   Spec. No. 1-10023 (N).   Neg. No. 5968.

EXPLANATION OF PLATE XXXV.

Stone mortars and metates.

Figure 1. Small stone mortar. Spec. No. 1-9974 (N). Neg. No. 5969.

Figure 2. Small stone mortar. Spec. No. 1-9912 (N). Neg. No. 5969.

Figure 3. Small stone mortar. Length 168 mm. Spec. No. 1-10011 (N). Neg. No. 5969.

Figure 4. Metate of Mono type. Spec. No. 1-10086 (C). Neg. No. 5974.

Figure 5. Metate of Mono type. Length 431 mm. Spec. No. 1-10191 (C). Neg. No. 5974.

EXPLANATION OF PLATE XXXVI.

Soaproot brushes used as meal and hair brushes.

Figure 1. Soaproot leaves bound with a twig and ready for the application of soaproot juice or pitch to make the handle. Spec. No. 1-9954 (N).

Figure 2. Soaproot brush in prime condition. Spec. No. 1-9926 (N).

Figure 3. Soaproot brush made of fibers bound with string but not held together by any adhesive agent. Spec. No. 1-10176 (C).

Figure 4. New soaproot brush, showing newly applied soaproot juice to make handle. Spec. No. 1-10245 (S).

Figure 5. Very old and much worn soaproot brush. Length 123 mm. Spec. No. 1-9955 (N).

Figure 6. Soaproot brush. Spec. No. 1-10268 (C).

Figure 7. Very old soaproot brush. Spec. No. 1-9973 (N). *Neg. No. 5966.*

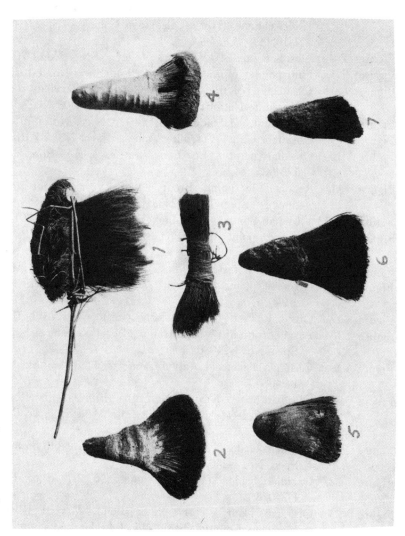

EXPLANATION OF PLATE XXXVII.

Obsidian and Flint Points.

Figure 1. Basal portion of arrow point. Excavated just northeast of Mineral Station, about five miles east of Mokelumne Hill, Calaveras County. Spec. No. 1-10509.

Figures 2–4. Obsidian points. Yosemite Valley. Spec. No. 1-7013.

Figure 5. Flint point. (Location same as 1.) Spec. No. 1-10509.

Figures 6, 7. Obsidian points. Big Meadow, Coulterville road, Yosemite National Park. Spec. No. 1-24083, 1-24084.

Figure 8. Flint point. (Location same as 1.) Spec. No. 1-10509.

Figure 9. Obsidian point. Yosemite Valley. Spec. No. 1-7013.

Figure 10. Obsidian point. (Location same as 6, 7.) Spec. No. 1-24085.

Figure 11. Reddish flint point. From site of Eyeyaku, near Tuolumne. Spec. No. 1-24331.

Figures 12, 13. Obsidian points. Yosemite Valley. Spec. No. 1-7013.

Figure 14. Obsidian point. (Location same as 11.) Spec. No. 1-24332.

Figure 15. Obsidian point. (Location same as 9.) Spec. No. 1-7013.

Figure 16. Obsidian point. (Location same as 6, 7.) Spec. No. 1-24081.

Figure 17. Obsidian point. (Location same as 9.) Spec. No. 1-7013.

Figure 18. Basal portion of obsidian blade. (Location same as 6, 7.) Spec. No. 1-24080.

Figure 19. Obsidian flake. (Location same as 6, 7.) Spec. No. 1-24086.

Figure 20. Obsidian blade. Near top of S-turn, Big Oak Flat Road, at 4900 feet elevation, Yosemite Valley. Spec. No. 1-18584.

Figure 21. Obsidian blade. (Location same as 6, 7.) Length 85 mm. Spec. No. 1-24079.

Figure 22. Obsidian blade. (Location same as 6, 7.) Spec. No. 1-24078.

Figure 23. Obsidian blade. Horse Shoe Bend, Merced River, Mariposa County. Spec. No. 1-4511.

Figure 24. Obsidian blade. (Location same as 6, 7.) Spec. No. 1-24077.

Neg. No. 8275.

BULL, PUBL. MUS., MILW.

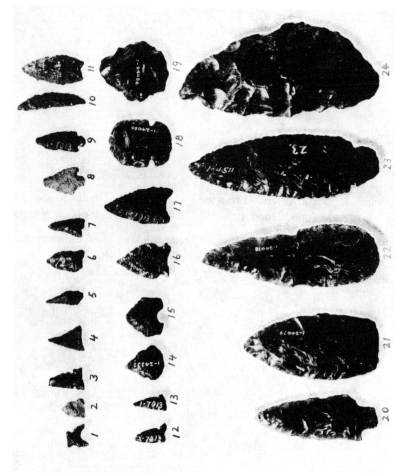

EXPLANATION OF PLATE XXXVIII.

Figure 1. Exterior and entrance of a subterranean dance house. Near Ione, Amador County. Northern Miwok. Neg. No. 8590.

Figure 2. Interior of above dance house, looking from doorway across fireplace to rear wall. Neg. No. 1619.
Photos: Courtesy of Hugh W. Littlejohn.

2

1

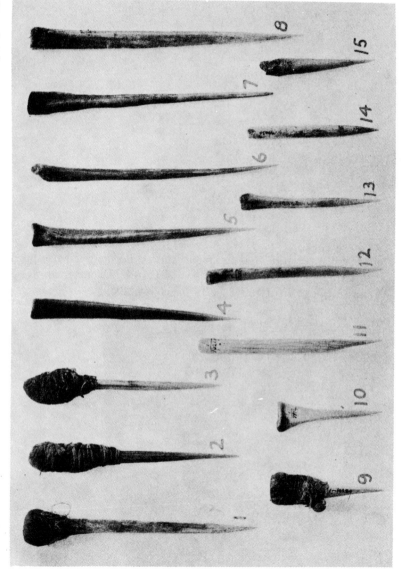

EXPLANATION OF PLATE XL.

Coiled basket, of three-rod technique and of northern type, especially used by chiefs for serving foods at feasts. Diameter at rim 708 mm. Spec. No. 1-10282 (C). Neg. No. 4969.

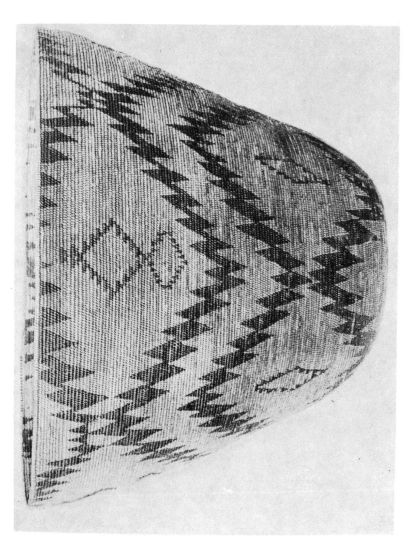

303

EXPLANATION OF PLATE XLI.

Coiled basket, of multiple-grass technique, and of southern type, pattern of Yokuts type. Diameter at rim 631 mm. Spec. No. 1-410 (S). Neg. No. 5971.

305

EXPLANATION OF PLATE XLII.

Coiled cooking baskets of three-rod technique.

Figure 1. Spec. No. 1-10156 (C).

Figure 2. Spec. No. 1-9949 (C). Shows repair, especially at bottom.

Figure 3. Spec. No. 1-9952 (C).

Figure 4. Spec. No. 1-10265 (S). Diameter at rim 612 mm. *Neg. No. 4875.*

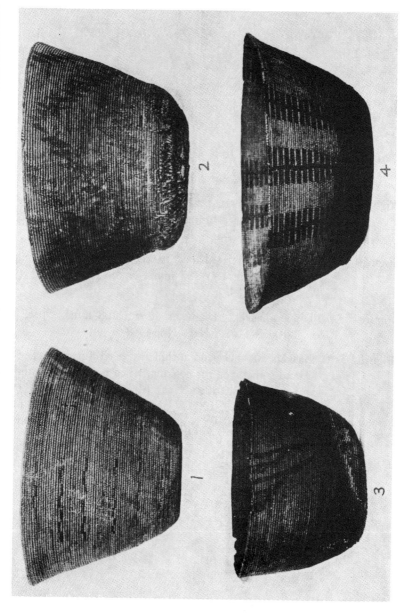

1

2

3

4

307

308

EXPLANATION OF PLATE XLIV.

Coiled cooking baskets of three-rod technique.

Figure 1. Spec. No. 1-10059 (N).
Height 175 mm.

Figure 2. Spec. No. 1-10175 (C).

Figure 3. Spec. No. 1-10185 (C).

Figure 4. Spec. No. 1-10288 (C).

Figure 5. Spec. No. 1-10264 (S).

Figure 6. Spec. No. 1-10124 (C).
Neg. No. 4876.

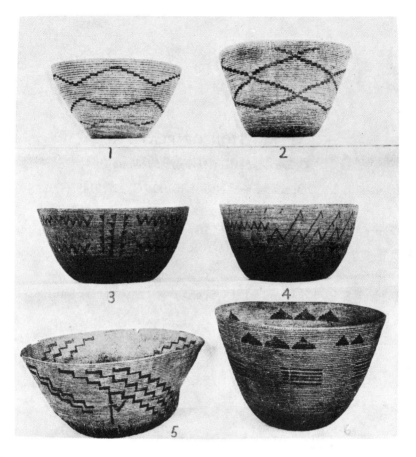

EXPLANATION OF PLATE XLV.

Coiled baskets of three-rod technique.

Figures 1, 2. Dippers. Spec. Nos. 1-10100 (C), 1-10149 (C). No. 2, height 162 mm.

Figure 3. General receptacle, especially for serving food. Spec. No. 1-10294 (C).

Figure 4. Globose basket. Spec. No. 1-10194 (C).

Figures 5, 6. Cooking basket. Spec. Nos. 1-9972 (N), 1-10106 (C). *Neg. No. 4878.*

EXPLANATION OF PLATE XLVI.

Coiled baskets of three-rod technique, used as general receptacles, especially for serving food.

Figure 1. Spec. No. 1-9935 (N).

Figure 2. Spec. No. 1-10184 (C).
Height 150 mm.

Figure 3. Spec. No. 1-9920 (N).

Figure 4. Spec. No. 1-10067 (C).
Neg. No. 5972.

316

EXPLANATION OF PLATE XLVIII.

Coiled baskets of single-rod technique.

Figure   1.   Dipper Basket. Spec. No. 1-9911 (N). Neg. No. 4972. Diameter at rim 201 mm.

Figure   2.   Parching basket. Spec. No. 1-10261 (S). Neg. No. 4972.

Figure   3.   Elliptical or canoe-shaped basket. Spec. No. 1-10153 (C). Neg. No. 4877. Diameter at rim 416 mm.

Figures 4, 5.   Basket used for serving food and as general receptacles. Spec. Nos. 1-10203 (C), 1-10158 (C). Neg. No. 4877.

Figure   6.   Hemispherical basket. Spec. No. 1-10107 (C). Neg. No. 4877.

Figure   7.   Basket used as a general receptacle and for serving food. Spec. No. 1-10152 (C). Neg. No. 4877.

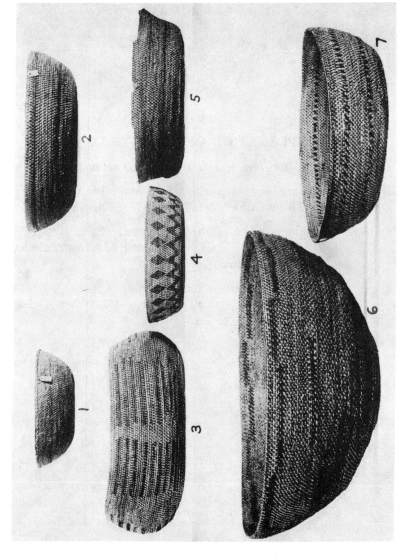

EXPLANATION OF PLATE XLIX.

Coiled plate-form baskets of single-rod technique.

Figure   1.   Basket used for parching seeds and other foods. Height 71 mm. Spec. No. 1-9910 (N). Neg. No. 5977.

Figures 2, 3.   Winnowing baskets for acorn meal. Spec. Nos. 1-9936 (N), 1-10088 (C). Neg. No. 4967. No. 2, diameter at rim 386 mm.

Figures 4, 5.   Winnowing baskets for acorn meal. Spec. Nos. 1-9901 (N), 1-10089 (C). Neg. No. 4971. No. 4, height 66 mm.

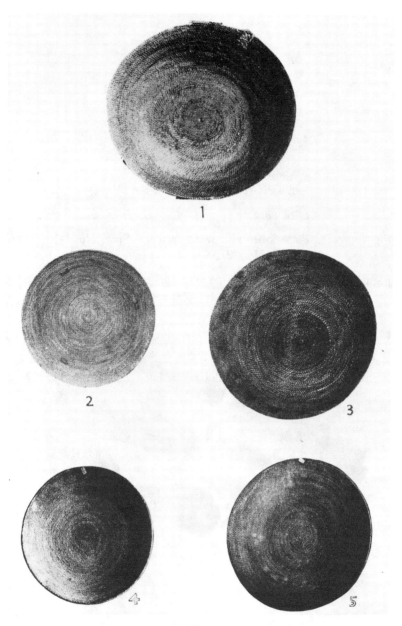

EXPLANATION OF PLATE L.

Coiled baskets of multiple-grass foundation.

Figure   1. Plate-form winnowing basket. Spec. No. 1-10155 (C).
                Neg. No. 8270.

Figure   2. Plate-form winnowing basket with herringbone border
                finish. Diameter 390 mm. Spec. No. 1-9936 (N).
                Neg. No. 8270.

Figures 3, 4. Dipper baskets. Spec. Nos. 1-10189 (C), 1-10260 (S).
                Neg. No. 8968. No. 3, height 111 mm.

Figure   5. Finely woven, globose basket. Spec. No. 1-10289 (C).
                Neg. No. 8968.

EXPLANATION OF PLATE LI.

Figure 1. Fire drill consisting of "hearth" and drill. Spec. No. 1-10623 (C). Neg. No. 5967. Length of "hearth" 213 mm.

Figure 2. Coiled basket with split stitch on exterior only. Indian Creek, Calaveras County. Specimen 74928 (C), Peabody Museum, Harvard University.

Figure 3. Seed beater resembling Cahuilla type of southern California. Northern Miwok, Amador County. Spec. No. 63424, Peabody Museum, Harvard University. Length 460 mm.

Courtesy: Peabody Museum, Harvard University.

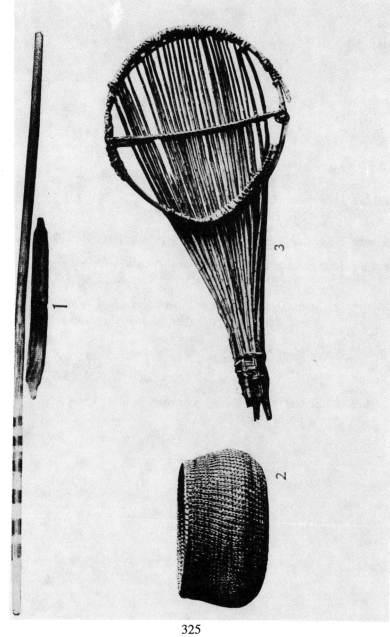

EXPLANATION OF PLATE LII.

Openwork baskets of plain twined technique.

Figure 1. Sifter. Length 400 mm. Spec. No. 1-10000 (N). Neg. No. 5970.

Figure 2. Sifter. Spec. No. 1-10123 (C). Neg. No. 5970.

Figure 3. Seed beater used with burden basket for harvesting seeds. Spec. No. 1-10145 (C). Neg. No. 5970.

Figure 4. Sifter. In this specimen the courses of twining pass back and forth close together, so that they appear like braiding. Diameter at rim 378 mm. Spec. No. 1-10237 (S). Neg. No. 5973.

Figure 5. Sifter. Spec. No. 1-10140 (C). Neg. No. 5973.

Figure 6. Sifter, very old and showing repairs. Spec. No. 1-9971 (N). Neg. No. 5973.

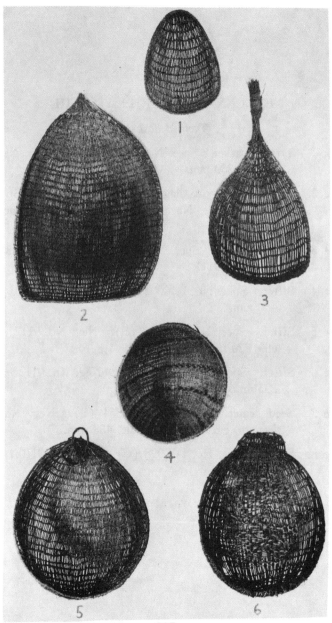

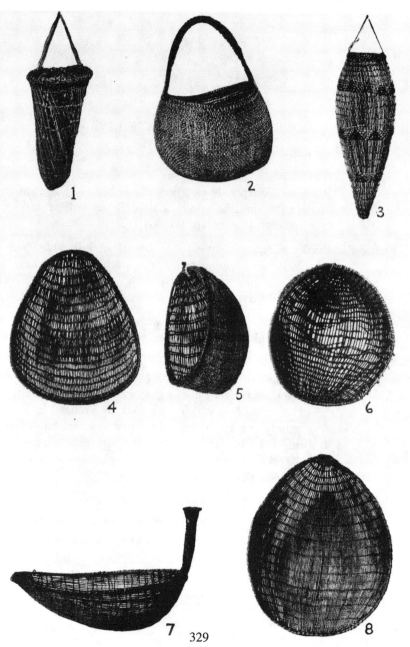

EXPLANATION OF PLATE LIV.

Burden baskets of twined techniques.

Figure 1. Burden basket, illustrating viz. (1) beginning by bending ends of warp rods together, (2) bands of close twining near the rim, the lower band partly of redbud bark to give color. Spec. No. 1-10069 (C).

Figure 2. Burden basket without coating of soaproot juice. Only suitable for carrying coarser things, such as acorns. Point repaired and strengthened with rawhide. Spec. No. 1-10248 (S).

Figure 3. Burden basket newly coated with soaproot juice, applied within and without to render it tight to hold small seeds. Spec. No. 1-10239 (S).

Figure 4. Burden basket, illustrating viz: (1) beginning with crossed warp elements, (2) use of grape vine at bottom and top, (3) rim finish in which warp rods are grouped in fours, but only one rod is bent over to form rim, the others being cut off. Diameter at rim 538 mm. Spec. No. 1-10094 (C).
Neg. No. 8271.

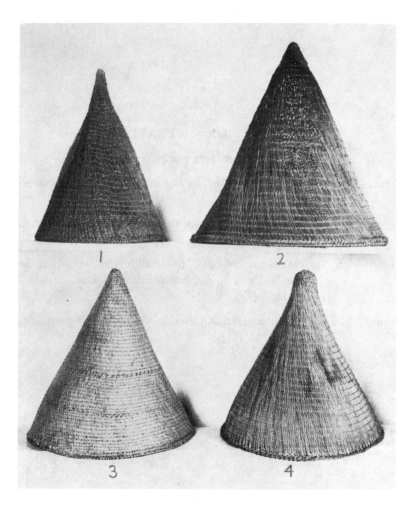

EXPLANATION OF PLATE LV.

Basket rackets and balls.

Figures 1, 2. Basket rackets used in women's ball game. Spec. No. 1-10363 (C). Fig. 1, length 422 mm.

Figures 3, 4. Wooden balls used in men's game of shinney. Spec. No. 1-10356 (S).

Figure   5. Buckskin-covered ball used with the basket rackets, figures 1 and 2, in the women's ball game. Spec. No. 1-10362 (C).

Figure   6. Buckskin-covered ball used in the men's ball game. Spec. No. 10361 (C).
Neg. No. 5976.

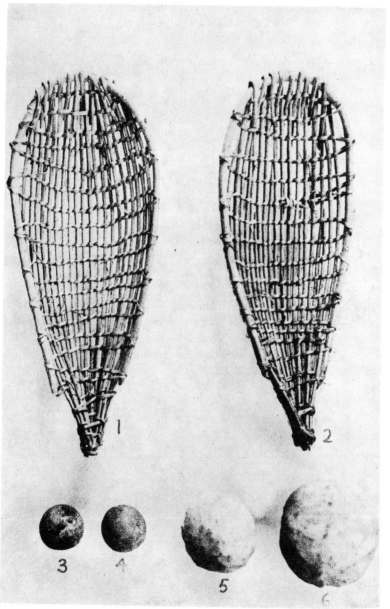

EXPLANATION OF PLATE LVI.

Tubular pipes.

Figure   1.   Tubular pipe of elder with pith removed.   Length 111 mm.   Spec. No. 1-10359 (S).

Figures 2–4.   Tubular pipes of wood. Spec. Nos. 1-10307 (C), 1-10358 (S), 1-10134 (C).

Figures 5–12. Tubular pipes from the Yokuts living immediately to the south.   These are shown for purposes of comparison.   Spec. Nos. 1-10761, 1-3960, 1-10800, 1-3961, 1-9169, 1-10870, 1-3962, 1-4083.
Neg. No. 4825.

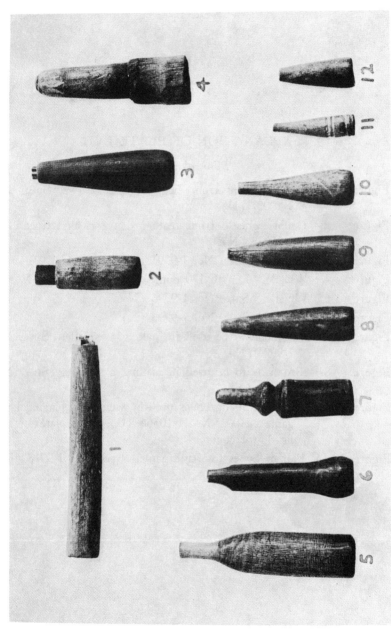

EXPLANATION OF PLATE LVII.

Bone objects.

Figure   1. Double whistle from feather dance cloak. Spec. No. 1-10037 (N).

Figure   2. Double whistle from feather dance cloak. Spec. No. 1-10038 (N).

Figure   3. Whistle. Spec. No. 1-9991 (N).

Figure   4. Whistle. Length 170 mm. Spec. No. 1-9992 (N).

Figure   5. Whistle. Spec. No. 1-9996 (N).

Figure   6. Whistle. Spec. No. 1-9993 (N).

Figure   7. Bird bone to be used in making a whistle. Spec. No. 1-9994 (N).

Figure   8. Bird bone to be used in making a whistle. Spec. No. 1-9995 (N).

Figures 9-12. Set of gambling bones used by women in playing hand game. Spec. No. 1-10364 (C). See plate LVIII, fig. 1, for counters.

Figures 13-14. Pair of bones for hand game. Spec. No. 1-9918 (N). *Neg. No. 8273.*

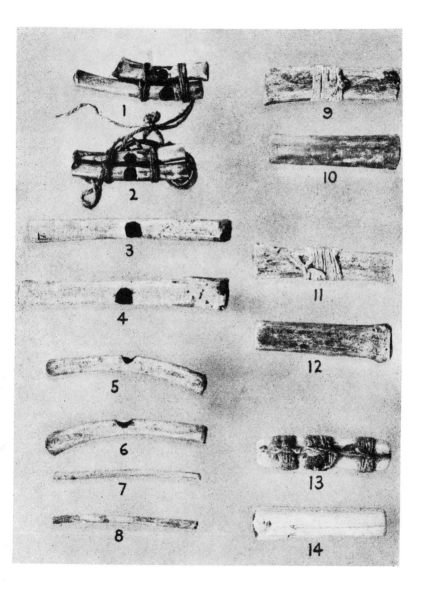

EXPLANATION OF PLATE LVIII.

Bone and wooden objects.

Figure   1.   Eight wooden counters used with bones in plate LVII, figs. 9-14. Spec. No. 1-10365 (C).

Figures 2, 3.   Mesh sticks for making hair net. Spec. Nos. 1-9990 (N) and 1-9988 (N). Fig. 3, length, 135 mm.

Figure   4.   Mesh sticks for net making. Spec. No. 1-10022 (N).

Figure   5.   Same as fig. 3. Spec. No. 1-9989 (N).

Figure   6.   Same as fig. 3. Spec. No. 1-9987 (N).

Figures 7-10.   Leg bones of deer, partly worked and polished, to be used in making gambling bones. Spec. Nos. 1-9984 (N), 1-9983 (N), 1-9986 (N), and 1-9985 (N).

Figure   11.   Deer antler implement, used to extract acorns from the bark of trees, where they had been placed by woodpeckers. Spec. No. 1-9968 (N).
Neg. No. 8272.

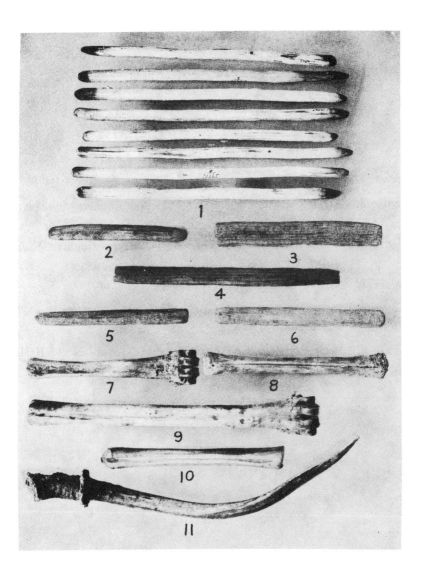

EXPLANATION OF PLATE LIX.

Figure 1. Sinew-backed bow, Calaveras County. Spec. No. 1-4488.

Figure 2. Arrow, with obsidian point, Calaveras County. Spec. No. 1-4490.

Figure 3. Arrow, formerly with flint point, Calaveras County. Spec. No. 1-4489.

Figure 4. Arrow, Calaveras County. Spec. No. 1-4491.

Figure 5. Digging stick for bulbs and roots. Spec. No. 1-10019 (N). Length, 850 mm.

Figure 6. Mink skin headband used in dances. Spec. No. 1-10042 (N). Length, exclusive of strings, 640 mm.
Neg. No. 8276.

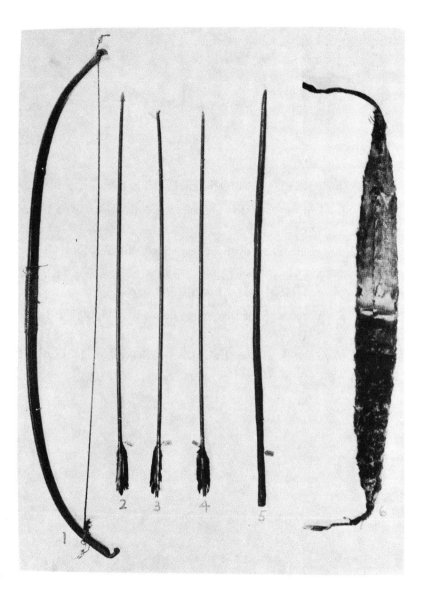

EXPLANATION OF PLATE LXI.

Jackrabbit-skin blanket. Width about 1700 mm. Obtained from Northern Miwok, but purchased by them from the Washo. Spec. No. 1-9919. Neg. No. 8278.

EXPLANATION OF PLATE LXII.

Figure 1. Summer moccasin, showing mended sole. Spec. No. 1-10129b (C). Length about 225 mm.

Figure 2. Summer moccasin. Spec. No. 1-10129a (C).

Figure 3. Cotton hair net. Spec. No. 1-9981 (N).

Figure 4. Cotton hair net. Spec. No. 1-10041 (N).
Neg. No. 8280.

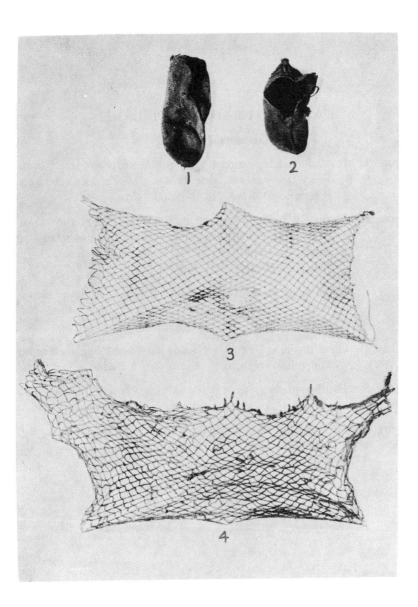

EXPLANATION OF PLATE LXIII.

Ceremonial Objects.

Figure 1. Invitation string, used to call people together for a ceremony; the knots indicate days to elapse before ceremony
commences. Spec. No. 1-10360 (N).

Figure 2. Mourning string tied about neck of mourner at funeral of
near relative; must remain there until it wears in two or
falls off, or until next annual mourning ceremony. Spec.
No. 1-9965 (N).

Figure 3. Paint stick; by charring end and rubbing directly on skin a
black design is produced. Length, 133 mm. Spec. No.
1-9982 (N).

Figure 4. Olive shells. *(Olivella biplicata)* used in making shell ropes
and other ornaments. Spec. No. 1-10159 (C).

Figure 5. Pouches made of the everted skin of a hawk's legs, used as
receptacles to store down. Spec. No. 1-10314 (C).

Figure 6. Long tubular bead of shell, worn as nose stick. Spec. No.
1-10195 (C).
Neg. No. 5978.

EXPLANATION OF PLATE LXIV.

Figure 1. Old magpie feather dance skirt, with pendant of flicker feather band and double bone whistle. West Point, Calaveras County. Cat. No. 10037 (N). Neg. No. 4772.

Figure 2. Old dance skirt of Great Horned Owl and hawk feathers, with pendant and double bone whistle. West Point, Calaveras County. Cat. No. 10038 (N). Neg. No. 4773.

351

EXPLANATION OF PLATE LXV.

Feather skirt. Back of 1-10038, shown in plate LXIV, fig. 2, showing manner of attaching feathers, length about 902 mm. Neg. No. 8279.

Rope of olive shells. Length of ten shells, 220 mm. Spec. No. 1-20885, Calaveras County. Neg. No. 8277.

EXPLANATION OF PLATE LXVII.

Cat's cradle. Representations of sky, clear and cloudy. Central Miwok.

Figure   1.   Start. Neg. No. 7131.

Figure   2.   Second stage. Neg. No. 7132.

Figures 3, 4.   Third stage, cloudy sky. Neg. Nos. 7133, 7134.

Figures 5, 6.   Fourth stage, clearing sky. Neg. Nos. 7135, 7136.

Figures 7, 8.   Fifth stage, clear sky. Neg. Nos. 7137, 7138.

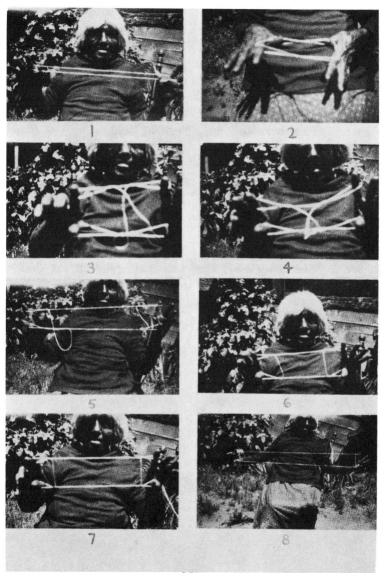

EXPLANATION OF PLATE LXVIII.

Cat's Cradle. Central Miwok.

Figure 1. Flea, ready to jump. Neg. No. 7140.

Figure 2. Flea, jumping. Neg. No. 7141.

Figure 3. Stealing (wüla), preliminary. Neg. No. 7142.

Figure 4. Stealing (wüla), pulling string. Neg. No. 7143.

Figure 5. Stealing (wüla), pulling string, farther advanced. Neg. No. 7144.

Figure 6. Fish net (laso), before completing by turning over right hand. Neg. No. 7153.

Figure 7. Fish net (laso), completed by turning over right hand. Neg. No. 7154.

Figure 8. Fish net (laso), complete, and stretched somewhat. Neg. No. 7155.

EXPLANATION OF PLATE LXIX.

Cat's Cradle. Central Miwok.

Figure   1. Gopher (sowatü) or mole (tumilü), just before releasing string from thumb. Neg. No. 7145.

Figure   2. Gopher (sowatü) or mole (tumilü), string released from thumb and pulled, causing it to come from fingers. Neg. No. 7146.

Figure   3. Bark house (umutca), preliminary stage. Neg. No. 7156.

Figure   4. Bark house (umutca), complete. Neg. No. 7157.

Figures 5, 6. Girl baby (eselu osa), complete. Neg. Nos. 7151, 7152.

Figure   7. Boy baby (eselu naña), preliminary stage. Neg. No. 7147.

Figure   8. Boy baby (eselu naña), complete. Neg. No. 7150.

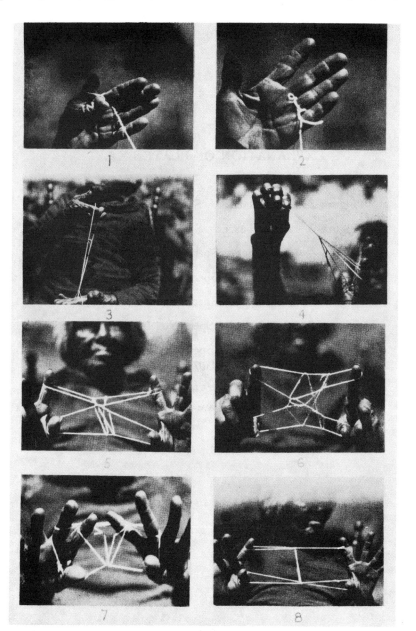

EXPLANATION OF PLATE LXX.

Figure 1. Acorn buzzer. Spec. No. 1-2267.

Figure 2. Acorn buzzer. Spec. No. 1-10600.

Figure 3. Acorn buzzer. Spec. No. 1-10137 (C).

Figure 4. Acorn top. Spec. No. 1-10139 (C).

Figure 5. Acorn top. Spec. No. 1-10035 (N).

Figure 6. Acorn top. Spec. No. 1-10135 (C).

Figure 7. Acorn dice. Spec. No. 1-10603.

Figure 8. Acorn dice. Spec. No. 1-10602.
Neg. No. 4807.

(Figures 1 and 2 are, respectively, Sinkyone and Pomo, included for comparison. Figures 7 and 8 are Pomo, but represent the Miwok equally well.)

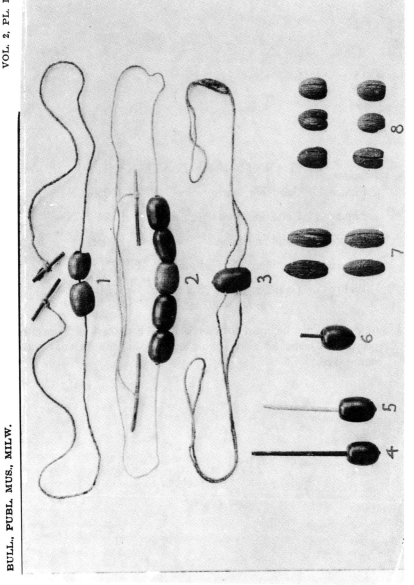

(Figure 3 is Yokuts, included for comparison. Figures 4 and 5 are, respectively, Chemeluevi and Yokuts and are shown in lieu of Miwok walnut dice.)

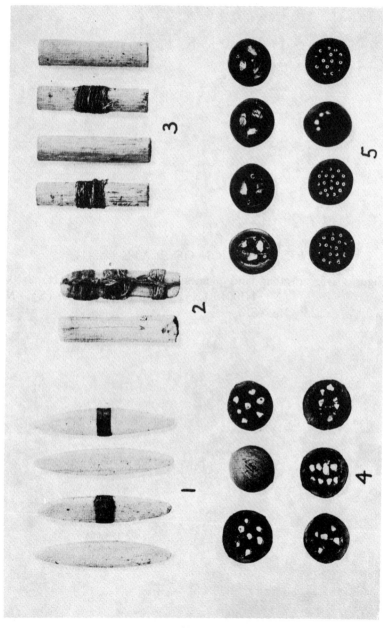

EXPLANATION OF PLATE LXXII.

Figures 1-5.   Feather dance plumes. Spec. Nos. 1-10047 (N), 1-10043 (N), 1-10045 (N), 1-9978 (N), 1-10229 (S).   Neg. No. 4813.

EXPLANATION OF PLATE LXXIII.

Figures 1-3. Flicker quill headbands. Spec. Nos. 1-14540, 1-10039 (N), 1-10040 (N). Neg. No. 5000.

(Figure 1 is Wintun, included for comparison.)

1   2   3

EXPLANATION OF PLATE LXXIV.

Figures 1–4. Cradles. Spec. Nos. 1-10119 (C), 1-10057 (N), 1-10055 (N), 1-10259 (S). Neg. No. 4880.

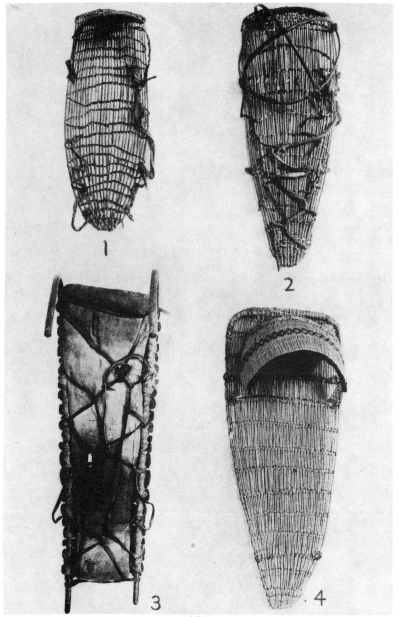

1

2

3

4

EXPLANATION OF PLATE LXXV.

Figures 1-4.   Cradles. Spec. Nos. 1-10216 (S), 1-10235 (S), 1-10944 (Western Mono), 1-10731 (Maidu).   Neg. No. 5003.

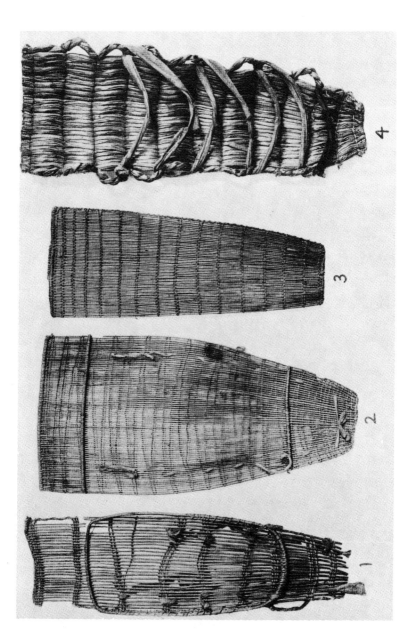

EXPLANATION OF PLATE LXXVI.

Figures 1, 2. Sections of one pack strap. Spec. No. 1-20894 (C).
Neg. No. 8273.

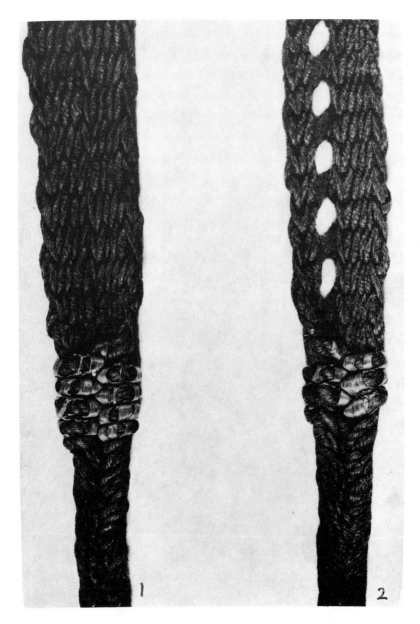

NOTES

NOTES

NOTES

NOTES

NOTES

NOTES

NOTES

NOTES

NOTES

NOTES

NOTES

NOTES

NOTES